ENGLISH WORKS

ON THE PHONE

LESLIE ROFE

PETER STRUTT

GRAHAM BUSHNELL

BELIN
8 RUE FÉROU, 75278 PARIS CEDEX 06

ISBN 2-7011-1110-2

TABLE DES MATIÈRES

INTRODUCTION

English Works on the Phone comporte un livret et deux cassettes. L'ensemble est conçu pour vous permettre

• d'améliorer votre compréhension de l'anglais parlé — le téléphone pose souvent un problème aux personnes qui ont l'habitude d'avoir un interlocuteur en face d'elles ou un texte sous les yeux.

• d'élargir votre vocabulaire pour tout ce qui concerne le téléphone : conversation, services téléphoniques, technologie et matériel des télécommunications.

CONTENU DU LIVRET

Il y a 10 unités, précédées par une brève histoire du téléphone. Chaque unité (à l'exception de Unit 10 qui sert de révision) traite d'une fonction linguistique liée à l'utilisation du téléphone et comporte non seulement des exercices de compréhension orale mais aussi des documents authentiques, des exercices de compréhension écrite et des jeux de rôles. A la fin du livret se trouvent les 'Tapescripts' (voir page 5), les 'Part B' (les instructions pour les jeux de rôles ; voir page 5), un corrigé de tous les exercices, et un glossaire des mots et expressions qui apparaissent dans le livret et qui relèvent du langage des communications téléphoniques.

CONTENU DES CASSETTES

Chaque unité commence par une ou plusieurs activités fondées sur des conversations téléphoniques enregistrées sur cassette. Le symbole  indique un texte enregistré. Au total 20 conversations sont enregistrées.

HOW TO USE A UNIT

LISTENING COMPREHENSION

• With the exception of Units 5, 6 and 10, each Unit contains the text of a recorded telephone conversation with blanks to be filled in by the student. Translations of the missing words and phrases are provided as a guide. The student may wish to attempt the blank-fill before listening to the cassette and then check his or her answers with the recording. Alternatively, the teacher may choose to play the cassette, books closed, for general comprehension before the students attempt the blank-fill. Answers are provided in the 'corrigé' at the back of the book.
• With the exception of Units 1, 3 and 7, there are recorded conversations which are accompanied by comprehension activities other than 'blank-fill'. In this case, the heading **Comprehension** precedes the activity. The answers can be found in the 'corrigé', and the tapescripts of the recorded conversations appear in the section entitled **Tapescripts.**

READING COMPREHENSION

The listening comprehension activities are followed by reading comprehension activities entitled **Practice**, based on authentic or semi-authentic documents giving information about different 'telephone services'. The answers to these exercises can be found in the 'corrigé'.

ROLE-PLAY

The heading **Do it yourself** precedes instructions for pair-work/role-play in the classroom (with the exception of Unit 6 where individual work is concerned). The student who chooses part **A** reads the instructions on the page of the unit. **B** turns to the section entitled **Part B** at the back of the book for his or her instructions. In this way, any preparation of a written script instead of an 'improvised' role-play is avoided.

LEXIQUE

This list includes those words and expressions in the book that specifically concern telephone language and services.

THE HISTORY OF THE TELEPHONE

SOME IMPORTANT DATES

• 1876: Alexander Graham Bell, a teacher of deaf children in Boston, patented the first telephone. The first words spoken over the phone were Bell's to his assistant: "Mr Watson, come here, I want you."

• 1877: Edison added a carbon transmitter to Bell's invention, giving a better sound reproduction over a longer distance.

• 1881: The first Post Office Telephone Exchange was opened in Swansea, Wales.

• 1891: The first telephone cable linking Paris and London was laid.

• 1892: The first long-distance call took place between New York and Chicago.

• 1901: Marconi transmitted the first radio signals across the Atlantic. In future, long distance phone calls and, later, TV broadcasts, were to be carried by radio wave technology.

• 1912: The British telecommunications system was nationalised.

• 1937: The "999" emergency service was introduced in Britain.

• 1956: The first transatlantic telephone cable was put into operation.

• 1962: Telstar, the first communications satellite, was launched.

• 1969: The GPO (General Post Office) ceased to be a government department and became a Corporation.

• 1976: The first optical cable system in Europe came into operation. A single hair-thin, glass fibre can carry over 8,000 telephone calls and can handle billions of calls a year.

1979: Prestel, the world's first public viewdata system, was launched in London. By this system, information held in computers can be transmitted via a telephone line and shown on a television screen.

• 1981: British Telecom, a separate public corporation providing telecommunication services, was created.

• 1984: British Telecom was privatised.

MAKING A CALL

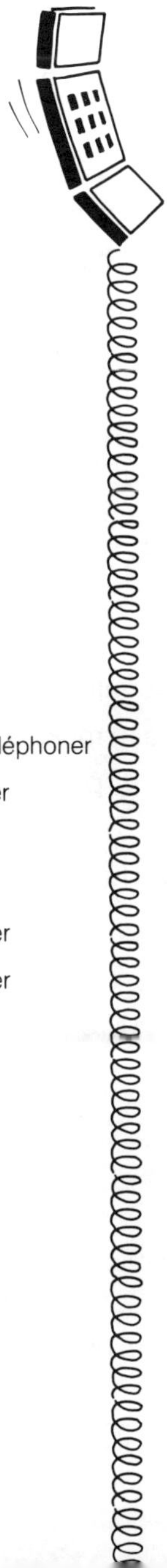

Molly is an American girl who has just arrived in England and is staying with an English family. It's her first visit to England and she wants to call home and tell her parents that she has arrived safely. Listen to her conversation with Mrs Evans and fill in the blanks. The numbered blanks represent missing words which are translated in the margin. The lettered blanks represent figures.

MRS EVANS : Right, dear. Is everything all right? Have you got everything you need in your room? I think I put you out a towel, didn't I?

MOLLY : Yes, thank you, Mrs Evans. Everything's fine. Er...but there is one thing.

MRS EVANS : What's that, love?

MOLLY : Well, I told my parents this morning that I'd ①_______________ this evening just to say that I had arrived safely. Do you mind if I use the telephone to ②_______________ to the States? I'll pay, of course.

① les appeler/leur téléphoner
② appeler/téléphoner

MRS EVANS : Oh no, that's no trouble. Um....The telephone's in the hall. Do you know how to ③_______________ to America ?

MOLLY : No, I've never ④_______________ before, well, in England, I mean.

③ appeler/téléphoner
④ appeler/téléphoner

MRS EVANS : Oh dear. Well, I'll give you a hand. Let's go into the hall. .....Right, now, what's your number in New York?

MOLLY : Um....it's A _______________

MRS EVANS : O.K., and what's the ⑤_______________

⑤ indicatif

MOLLY : Er.....it's included in the figures. All numbers in New York begin with B______

MRS EVANS : Oh, I see. Here you sometimes have other

⑥ chiffres

⑦ livret des indicatifs

⑧ combiné

⑨ tonalité

⑩ touches

⑪ cadran

⑫ occupé

⑬ occupé

⑭ raccrocher

⑮ rappeler

⑯ avoir la communication

⑰ central

⑱ opératrice

⑲ appel en PCV

⑳ appel en PCV

㉑ restez en ligne

㉒ vous passer la communication

⑥__________ in front of the number, too. If you live in London, it's C_____ In Manchester it's D______ and so on. Anyway, we've got to find the code for America. I'll look it up in the ⑦__________________________________ ....The United States....... Here we are! E________ . Right. Lift the ⑧______________ . That's it. Can you hear the ⑨________________ ?

MOLLY : Yes, I think so.

MRS EVANS : O.K. So press the ⑩__________ . Be careful not to press two at the same time. I prefer the old-fashioned ⑪______ myself. Is it ringing?

MOLLY : I don't think so. It sounds ⑫_______ .

MRS EVANS : Oh yes, it's ⑬__________ . Well, look... er... let's ⑭__________ a moment and we'll ⑮____________ in a minute or two.

....

MOLLY : I don't understand. I don't seem to be able to ⑯______________ .

MRS EVANS : Well, perhaps the ⑰____________ is saturated. I know what we'll do. We'll go through the ⑱____________ . Now, if we want to make a call to the States, I think there is a special number. Let me see... Here we are ! F______ .

MOLLY : Oh, by the way, I'd like my parents to pay for the call. I don't want you to have to pay.

MRS EVANS : Oh, it doesn't....

MOLLY : No, I insist.

MRS EVANS : Are you sure? Oh, all right. We'll ask for a ⑲____________________ call.

....

OPERATOR : International. What country?

MOLLY : The United States. I'd like to make a ⑳____________ ________ call to G_______________ please.

OPERATOR : What is your number, please?

MOLLY : Er.......What is the number here ?

MRS EVANS : H__________

MOLLY : I__________

OPERATOR : What town are you ringing from ?

MOLLY : Mallingham.

OPERATOR : Mallingham. Right, ㉑________________ and I'll try to ㉒____________________

MRS EVANS : I'll leave you to it.

MOLLY : O.K. Thank you very much.

OPERATOR : Hello, is that J____________ ? There's a call from England for you. Will you accept the charges?

THE TELEPHONE

SOME BASIC VOCABULARY

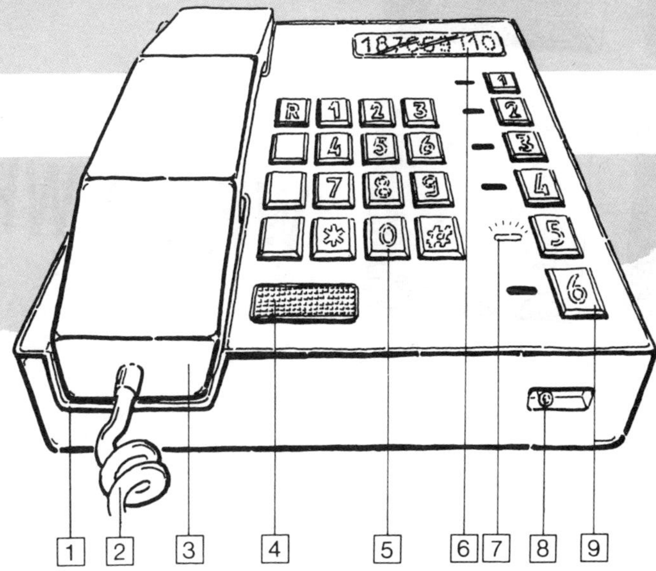

Practice

The numbers in the picture each represent a different part of the telephone. Match the numbers to the following words :

A. cord B. handset C. button D. digital display E. cradle F. socket G. loudspeaker
H. lamp I. extension lines.

Practice

Read the following passage and fill in the blanks using the words and expressions in the list below :

dial receiver switchboard hold on look up extension number tone
Directory Enquiries Yellow Pages directory area code handset

First, make sure you know the number you require and, where necessary, check the ____________ . If you are in any doubt, check them in the telephone ____________ and dialling code booklet. You can ________ the number of a business or organisation in the ____________ .

If you have to call ____________ , have a pen and paper ready to make a note of the number.

To make a call, first lift the ________ and listen for the dial ________ , a continuous purring or a high-pitched hum.

If necessary, ______ the code and then the number. If you have a press-button telephone, press each button carefully and avoid pressing two buttons at the same time.

If you make a mistake when dialling, replace the ________ for a moment or two, then start again.

After you have dialled, there may be a pause. ________ for about fifteen seconds (up to a minute for an international call) to allow the equipment time to make the connection.

When your call is answered, say who you want to talk to and then say who you are. If you are calling an organisation which has a ____________ , give the ____________ you require. If you do not know it, enquire and make a note of it for further use.

2 WHO ? WHAT ? WHERE ?

Comprehension

Listen to Conversation 1. A French businessman is phoning a British company. He gets through to the switchboard operator but ....

1. Why doesn't the switchboard operator understand the Frenchman properly ?
2. What is the probable outcome of their conversation ?

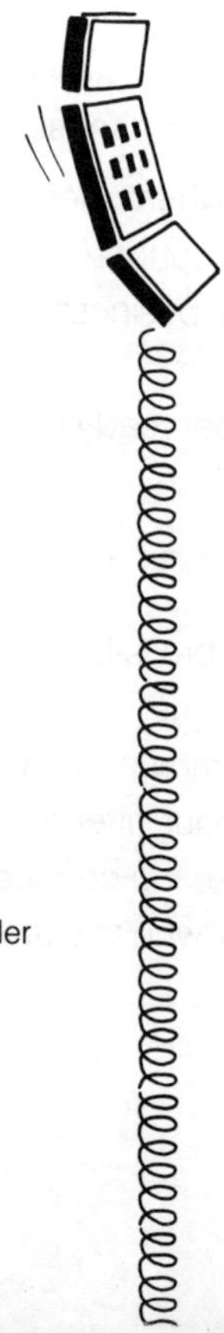

Listen to Conversation 2. Simon wants some information about a computer modem he has seen advertised. Fill in the blanks with the missing words and expressions. The numbered blanks are translated; the lettered blanks are not.

VOICE : Ilford 64521.

SIMON : Er..Is that Ilford Electronics?

VOICE : No, this is Geering's Newsagents.

SIMON : ① ______________________ .

VOICE : ② __________________________ .

① Désolé, c'est une erreur
② De rien

. . . .

WOMAN : Ilford Electronics. Can I help you?

SIMON : Yes, well, I hope so. I've read your advertisement in the magazine called...

WOMAN : I'm sorry, it's a bad line. ③ ______________________ ______________________ ?

③ Pourriez-vous parler un peu plus fort?

SIMON : O.K. I'll start again. I saw your advertisement in Personal

④ je me demandais

⑤ Pourriez-vous être plus précis ?

⑥ accéder à des banques de données

⑦ relié à un réseau

⑧ n'est-ce pas

⑨ A vrai dire

⑩ messagerie électronique

⑪ je ne sais pas ce que veut dire

⑫ c'est ça/n'est-ce pas

⑬ C'est ça.

⑭ voulez-vous que je

⑮ certainement

⑯ n'est-ce pas

⑰ à vrai dire

⑱ donnez-nous un coup de fil

Computer Weekly for the Skylark Modem and ④ ____________ ____________ if you could give me some more information about it.

WOMAN : Er...yes. What would you like to know? ⑤ ____________ ____________________________________?

SIMON : Well, I've got a BBC computer, and I'd like to be able be able to use it to ⑥ ____________________ and information services, er...home banking and so on.

WOMAN : Well, that's what a modem is for. What it does basically is to transform your computer into a terminal so you can then dial a telephone number and be ⑦ ____________________ such as Telecom Gold, Microlink, Micronet and a whole range of other services.

SIMON : Er...yes...Micronet. That's a sort of electronic magazine, ⑧ ____________ ?

WOMAN : That's right.

SIMON : Like Telecom Gold ?

WOMAN : Er...no. ⑨ ____________, Telecom Gold is different. If you've got a computer terminal connected to a telephone line, you can use the ⑩ ________________ facility, which is what Telecom Gold is, you see?

SIMON : Oh, I didn't know that. And..er..what's the price?

WOMAN : £74 with £3 for packing and postage. Oh, and you also get a free 16K ROM which enables you to download telesoftware.

SIMON : Er..I'm afraid ⑪ ____________________ "download telesoftware" ⑪ ____________ . Could you explain in simpler terms?

WOMAN : Oh, yes. What this means is that you can transfer programs and graphics down the telephone line into your own computer.

SIMON : I see. And that's included in the price, ⑫ ____________ ?

WOMAN : ⑬ ____________ . Look, er..⑭ ____________ send some documentation to you so you can see for yourself?

SIMON : Yes, ⑮ ____________ .

WOMAN : O.K. Could you give me your name and address?

SIMON : Yes, it's A____________________________________ ____

WOMAN : That's in Norfolk, ⑯ ____________ ?

SIMON : No ⑰ ____________ it's in Suffolk. And the post code is B____________ .

WOMAN : Right, I've got that. So, you should get the documentation within the next two or three days. And if there's anything else you want to know, just ⑱ ____________ .

SIMON : O.K. Thank you. Goodbye.

Emergency ! 999 !

When you are giving details over the phone, it is important to be able to say numbers and spell words with the correct pronunciation and phrasing. And when you call an emergency service, it is especially important.

Practice

1. Pronouncing the following individual letters often presents a problem. Practise saying them aloud. Each one is followed by a pronunciation 'clue' :

A rhymes with "day".
E rhymes with "tea".
I — the same as "eye".
Y — the same as "why".

G rhymes with "tea" and starts with the same sound as "judge".
J rhymes with "day" and starts with the same sound as "judge".

H starts with "A" (see above) and ends with the same sound as "chip".
K rhymes with "day".

R rhymes with "car".
V rhymes with "tea".
W is pronounced "double you".
X rhymes with "sex" !

2. When spelling out words, the use of an alphabet like the one below can help prevent misunderstandings. Over the phone we would say "A for Alfred, B for Benjamin", and so on.

A Alfred	G George	M Mary	S Samuel	Y Yellow
B Benjamin	H Harry	N Nellie	T Tommy	Z Zebra
C Charlie	I Isaac	O Oliver	U Uncle	
D David	J Jack	P Peter	V Victor	
E Edward	K King	Q Queen	W William	
F Frederick	L London	R Robert	X X-ray	

3. When giving telephone numbers, group them in twos or threes. In Britain, the figure "0" is pronounced like the letter "O", and as "zero" in North America. For a number such as 01 344 6697, we would say in Britain :

oh one..... three /double four......double six /nine seven

Practise saying these aloud :

• 061 44 362 • 02273 37691 • 0249 57200 • 021 897 4529

Do it yourself

PHONING IN AN EMERGENCY

There are four different situations in this activity. Each one involves phoning an emergency service or replying to an emergency call. Choose to be either A or B. If you are A, read the following instructions. If you are B, turn to page 48.

N.B. While A and B are talking, a third person should make a note of the time each call takes. Both speed and efficiency are essential.

A's instructions

1. You are the switchboard operator for the police emergency service. The phone has just rung. Answer it and say : "Police. Can I help you?" In order to send help to anyone, you need their name and number, their location and the location of the emergency.

2. There is smoke coming from the upstairs window of the house opposite yours. Your name is Frawley and you live at 35, Broughton Drive. Your telephone number is 1222 86711. You have rung the emergency services and have asked for the Fire Brigade. You are waiting for the Fire Brigade to answer.

3. You are the switchboard operator for the coastguard emergency service. The phone has just rung. Answer it and say : "Coastguard. Can I help you?" In order to send help, you need the caller's name, number, location and the location of the emergency.

4. You were walking home late this evening when you heard a cry from round the next corner. After hesitating for a few seconds, you walked slowly round the corner and saw a man lying, badly hurt, in a pool of blood. In the distance, two indistinct figures were running away. You have rung the emergency services from a nearby call box (number : 347 68990) and have asked for the police and the ambulance services. The operator is putting you through to the police who can deal with sending an ambulance as well. You are waiting for the police to answer. The map below shows you where you are, where the victim is, and in what direction you saw the two figures going.

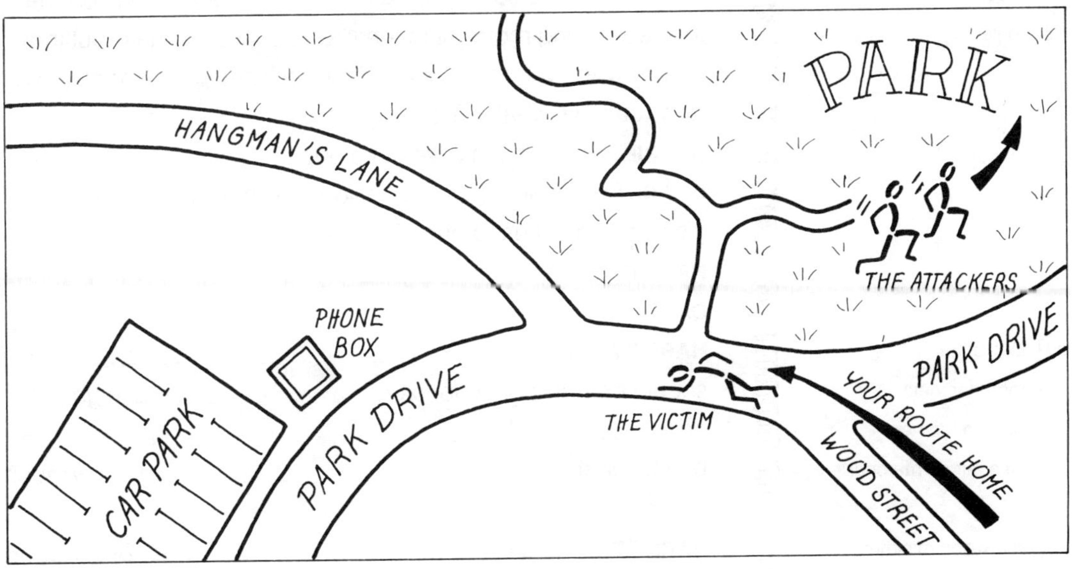

LOST !

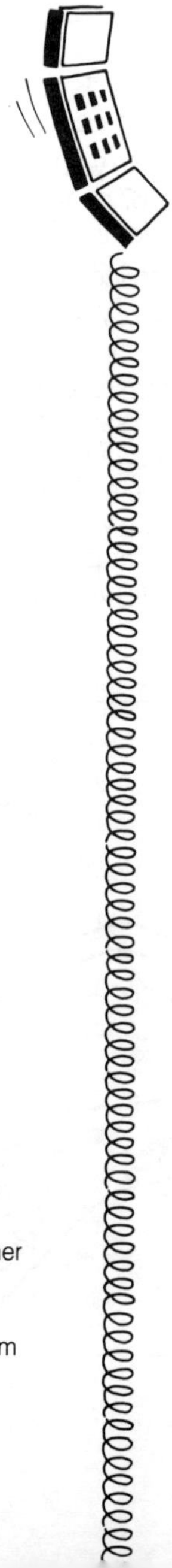

David and Harriet Spencer have been invited to Sunday lunch by their friends, Bill and Pamela Morgan, who they haven't seen for a long time and who now live about 30 miles away. Bill sent them a map a few days ago, showing them how to get there by car. David and Harriet set off half an hour ago but left the map at home by mistake . They have stopped at a phone box to get directions from Bill and Pamela. Listen to the conversation and fill in the blanks. The numbered blanks represent missing words which are translated in the margin. The lettered blanks are not translated.

① monnaie

DAVID : Have you got any ① __________ ? I've only got a five pound note.

HARRIET : Yes, I should have some in my purse. How much do you need?

② pièces
③ fente

DAVID : Give me some 10p ② ________ or 50p so we don't have to keep putting money into the ③ ________ . I hate putting in money when you're speaking. The other person keeps speaking and you miss what he's saying.

HARRIET : I don't think I've got a 50p...

DAVID : O.K. Well, give me what you have got. Now, what do I do? It's ages since I used one of these.

HARRIET : It says : "A ______________________ ".

DAVID : What ?

④ Décroche
⑤ ronronnement
⑥ bourdonnement
⑦ ça a l'air de marcher
⑧ la taxation minimum

HARRIET : ④ __________________________________ ! You should hear a "continuous ⑤ ______________ or a high-pitched ⑥ ________ ".

DAVID : Yeah, ⑦ ____________________________ . How much money do I put in ?

HARRIET : It says ⑧ _______________________ is 8p. Put in

⑨ Ça sonne?

⑩ ça n'a pas l'air

⑪ à l'appareil

⑫ cabine téléphonique

⑬ le signal sonore

⑭ On a été coupé

10p. Right, now dial.

DAVID : 8-2-6-1-9-5-5

HARRIET : ⑨ ________________ ?

DAVID : No ⑩ ______________________________ . What do I do now?

HARRIET : It says : "Press blue follow-on call button, listen for dial tone and call again." Press that button there. Right. Now dial again.

DAVID : Ah, that's better.

BILL : Whitstable 61955. Bill Morgan ⑪ __________ .

DAVID : Hello, Bill ! This is David.

BILL : David ! We were wondering where you'd got to !

DAVID : We're in a ⑫ ____________ just off the A299. We left the map at home by mistake, so it would help if you could tell us where to go from here!

BILL : Where are you exactly?

DAVID : We've just come off a roundabout and we're opposite a pub called The Prince of Wales.

BILL : Oh, yes. I see where you are. Well, listen. Go back on to the main road, heading towards B__________ , and after about C________________________ you come to another roundabout. O.K ? You take the D__________________________ and go down...er....it's called E______________ . And then you go F____________________ — it crosses the railway — and come to G________________ . Turn right, go H__________ __________ for about I__________________ and you'll see a J____________________ on your left. Turn left and......

DAVID : Oh hell ! There are ⑬ ____________ . Quick, Harriet, give me another 10p. Oh no ! ⑭ __________________ !

HARRIET : You should have put some more money in when you saw the red light flashing.

DAVID : Thank you very much ! We'll put in 30p this time.

....

DAVID : Sorry about that ! You were saying....

BILL : Yes. You turn left, go past the K________________ , a L________ club , then...er.....a gymnasium, and then at the first M________________ you turn right and you'll see the N______ ________________ in the middle of a square. You bear left and then go left again into O________________ . That's our street. We're at number 57 next door to a P______________ . On the Q__________________________ .

DAVID : O.K. I've got that. So, we'll see you in about 10 minutes. If we're not there by then, you'd better send out a search party !

BILL : O.K. David. See you in a few minutes.

THE PAYPHONE

THIS PAYPHONE ACCEPTS

2p 5p 10p 20p 50p £1

NO CHANGE GIVEN

If for example you insert a 50p coin and use less than 50p worth of time you will not receive change. Only wholly unused coins are returned. It is generally best for you to insert a mixture of coins including some low value coins. It is not advisable to use high value coins only, especially for short calls.

Have money ready: **Minimum fee — 8p**

1 Lift handset

Listen for dial tone. (Continuous purring or new dial tone: high-pitched hum).

2 Insert money

At least minimum fee. Credit display stops flashing on insertion of minimum fee.

Do not insert money for operators or SOS-Emergency (999) calls.

If dial tone stops before you start to dial, press blue follow-on call button, listen for dial tone, then dial number.

3 Dial number

Listen for ringing tone. Speak when connected.

4 Follow-on call

Failed call? New call with remaining credit? Do not replace handset. Press blue follow-on call button, listen for dial tone, then re-dial. (Minimum fee still applies. Insert more money if necessary.)

To continue a dialled call — when you see display flashing and hear paytone (rapid pips), or anytime during call, insert more money.

5 Replace handset

Collect refund. Part used coins are not returned so the refund may be less than the remaining credit.

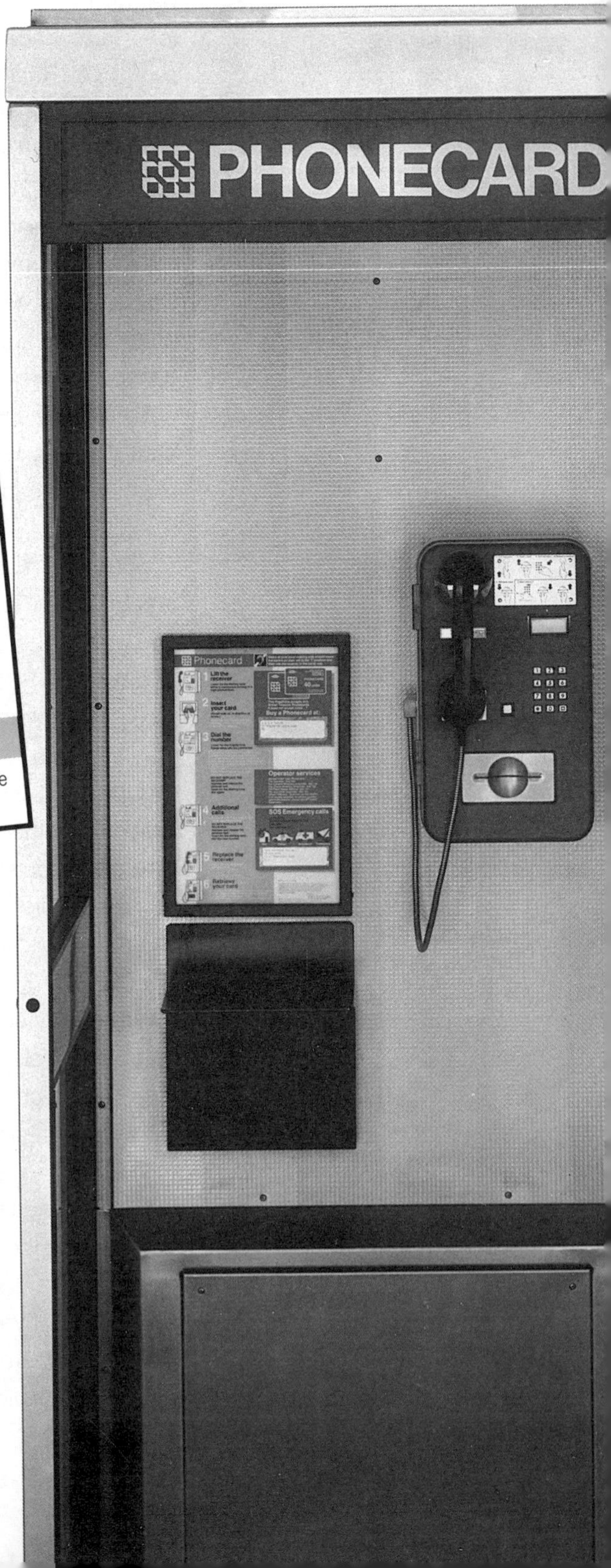

Practice

1. The instructions on this page are those found in the latest sort of British public phone box. Read them carefully and find the verbs which have the same meaning as the following "phrasal verbs" :

put in   pick up   give back   carry on   put through   put back

2. You have put in 30p and used 24p worth. You want to make a second call. What do you do?

3. You have put in 40p and used only 28p of your credit. Can you get the rest back?

Do it yourself

ASKING FOR DIRECTIONS

A is a student at a language school in England. B is a friend who has invited A to his/her house after class. A phones B to find out how to get there from the language school.
Choose your part (A or B). If you are A, read the following instructions. If you are B, **turn to page 49 for your instructions.**

A's instructions

You are at the language school (college). Your class has just finished. You know your friend lives at 30, Barton Close, but you don't know how to get there. Ring him/her up and ask for directions. Trace the route on the skeleton map below, indicating any landmarks.

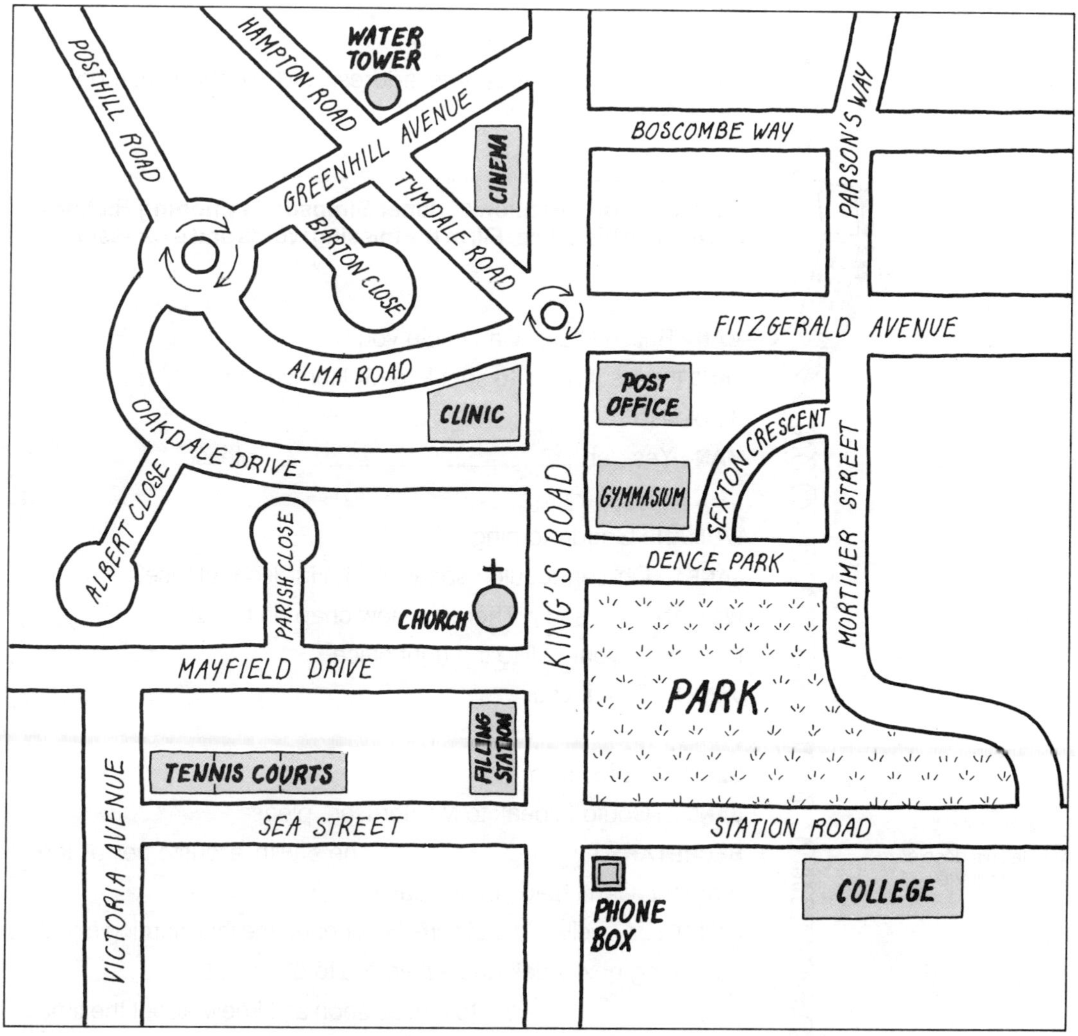

4 OPERATOR !

Comprehension

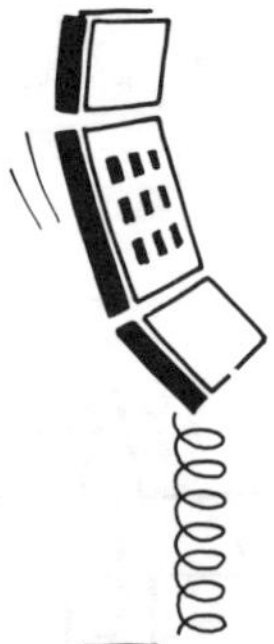

Listen to Conversation 1. A man is phoning Directory Enquiries to find out a phone number.

Write down the correct name, address and telephone number of the person in question.

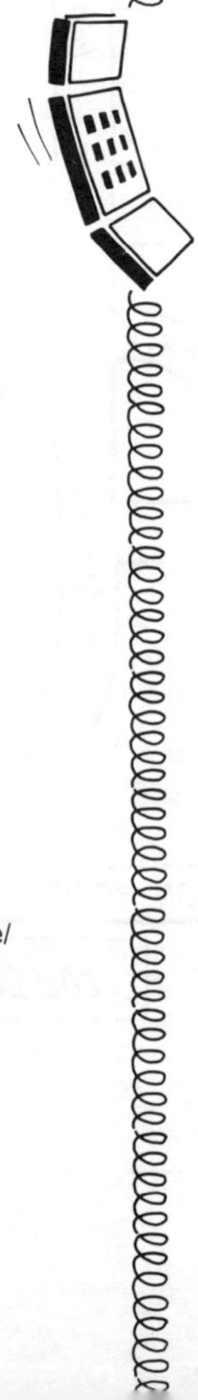

Listen to Conversation 2. Janet Simpson is phoning Richard Harrison at his office. Fill in the missing words and expressions.

MAN : British Glass. Can I help you?

① poste

JANET : Yes. I'd like to speak to Mr Harrison on ① __________ 34 please.

② ne quittez pas

MAN : Yes...er....② ____________________ please.

....

WOMAN : Good morning.

JANET : Oh...er...could I speak to Mr Harrison, please?

③ standard

WOMAN : Oh, sorry. There's a new chap on the ③ __________. I'll transfer your call to the right office.

JANET : Thank you.

....

SECRETARY : Hello.

JANET : Could I speak to Mr Harrison, please?

④ Je suis désolé/ Je regrette

SECRETARY : ④ ______________ he's with a customer at the moment. Can I help you instead?

⑤ recontacter

JANET : Er...well....I'm not sure. He phoned me this morning about a meeting next week and asked me to ⑤ ______________ ____________________ to him as soon as I knew about the time and place. He was also going to tell me of any items he wanted to be put on the ⑥ ________.

⑥ ordre du jour

⑦ transférer

SECRETARY : Oh....well, look, I'll ⑦ ____________ you to the office he's in. Wait a minute.

....

RICHARD : Hello.

JANET : Richard?

RICHARD : Speaking.

JANET : This is Janet. Sorry to interrupt you if you're busy, but I said I'd tell you where the meeting ⑧ ________________.

⑧ va avoir lieu

RICHARD : Yes, right.

JANET : Have you got a pen and paper ?

RICHARD : Yes, ⑨ ________________.

⑨ allez-y

JANET : The meeting is at Tube Investments in Detroit, at 9.30 on the 13th of March.....

VOICE : William? Is that you, William?

JANET : Is there anything you want to be brought up at the meeting?

VOICE : Who is this ? William?

RICHARD : The lines seem to be ⑩ ___________. Hello. Could you please get off the line !

⑩ embrouillées

VOICE : Who am I talking to?

RICHARD : Look, could you please hang up and call back? We have a problem with the lines. Sorry about that. Where were we?

JANET : Yes. Did you want to talk about anything special?

RICHARD : Sorry, Janet, but could you speak a bit louder? There seems to be a lot of ⑪ ______________ on the line.

⑪ parasites

JANET : Is there anything you particularly want to talk about at the meeting?

RICHARD : Er.....yes. I'd like to discuss the possibility of having a ⑫ __________________ the next time we have to meet. It seems to me we have to waste an enormous amount of time and money in travel and hotel accommodation when it would be so much simpler to stay in our own countries and talk to one another from a studio.

⑫ visioconférence

JANET : Good idea. I'll look into it.

RICHARD : There's a ⑬ _______________________ you can ring to get an idea of prices and times. It's 158. If you could get some facts and figures together we could make this a thing of the future.

⑬ numéro vert

JANET : Right. ⑭ ________. I'll leave you to your customer now.

⑭ Entendu

RICHARD : O.K. Janet. ⑮ _______________________.

⑮ Merci de votre appel

OPERATOR SERVICES

The British Telecom operators are there to help if you are having difficulty with a call, and can offer you the following range of services. Dial 100 for :

- **Alarm Calls**

If you've got to catch a very early plane or train maybe to go on holiday or if you've got an interview for a job, it's easy to oversleep or get so engrossed in what you are doing that you don't notice time passing. An alarm call is a sure way of alerting you at the time you want to be called. Alarm calls can be booked with the operator (preferably before 10.30pm the previous evening for an early morning call). You will be asked for the time you want to be called and your number. There is a charge for this service.

- **Freefone**

Freefone callers ask the operator to connect them with the Freefone name or number they require. There is no charge to the caller ; the Freefone subscriber pays the bill. The service is good for business ; it encourages people to communicate, the costs are reasonable and if your company has a Freefone name or number it can be listed in the telephone directory.

- **Advice of Duration and/or Charge**

Say you are making a call from another company's office and you want to pay them for it. Ask the operator to advise you of the charge ADC for short when you book the call. The operator will also give you the duration of the call if requested. The operator will ring back to tell you once you have finished your call. This service is charged.

- **Credit Card Calls**

A convenient way to call now and pay later. The credit card service means that you can make calls from any British Telecom phone, including coinboxes, without having to pay immediately.
Credit card calls are charged to your account and the service can be used both for Inland and international calls. They can also be made from some other countries to the UK.
There is a charge for each card and a fee for each call. Charges from abroad are usually the same as an operator call from the UK to the overseas country in question.

- **Transferred Charge Calls**

If you are short of change or using someone else's telephone, you can ask the operator to transfer the charges. The cost of the call is transferred to the number called, provided it is accepted when the operator speaks to the number called.
These calls can be made to you from many countries. In the majority of cases, the charges are the same as UK outgoing personal calls to that country, but in some cases they are higher.

Practice

Read the above extract from a British Telecom brochure, and say whether the following statements are true or false. Give your reasons.

1. None of the operator services mentioned is free.
2. You can't book an early morning call after 10.30pm in the evening.
3. A credit card call costs a little more than a normal call.
4. Freefone subscribers are usually companies.
5. You use the ADC service when you want someone else to pay for the call you are making.
6. If you want to transfer the charges, all you have to do is ask the operator to do so.

Do it yourself

ASKING FOR INFORMATION

A is a songwriter who is phoning the Royalties Manager of his/her publisher. B works in the royalties department. Choose your part (A or B). If you are A, read the following instructions. **If you are B, turn to page 50.**

A's instructions

You have had a collection of songs and music published. You receive a royalty on sales. However, you have not received a royalty statement or a cheque for the period ending 30th September, and it's already 5th October. The last statement you received was dated 30th March (see below). You are phoning the Royalties Manager to find out what has happened. You feel that either the statement and the cheque have been sent and have gone astray or, worse, the publisher may not have sent them at all ! Work out exactly what you will say from the following chart :

- Ask to speak to Mr Callan, the Royalties Manager.
- Introduce yourself. State briefly the reasons for your call.
- Describe the problem.
- Ask questions, e.g. How many copies sold? How much earned? Statement sent? If so, when?
- Thank your correspondent. Ring off.

EGBDF MUSIC LTD

A/C N°: M0075414
Date 30 March

Statement of account

Royalty description	Copies sold	Royalty rate	Payable
Songs and Music for the Fireside	2972	7%	£458.12

CAN I TAKE A MESSAGE ?

Comprehension

Listen to Conversation 1. Someone is calling the Manchester Exhibition Centre.

Fill in the missing details on the switchboard operator's message pad.

Date : 4TH MARCH
Time : 12.45.
Message for :
Caller's name :
Tel : EXT: 54.

MESSAGE

Re: ESTIMATE FOR NEW SWITCHBOARD
SENT AGO.
MR. REQUIRES DECISION
QUICKLY BECAUSE

Comprehension

Listen to Conversation 2. The switchboard operator has just finished writing the above message when the phone rings again.

Using the above message pad as a model, write down the next 5 messages.

INTERCOM T16

version luxe

Les fonctions classiques de l'intercommunication

• L'accès individuel à toutes les lignes extérieures du réseau téléphonique (jusqu'à 8 lignes réseau).

• La prise d'une communication à partir de n'importe quel poste de l'installation (jusqu'à 16 postes).

• L'établissement de communications intérieures entre les postes de l'installation.

• La possibilité de mettre en attente un correspondant extérieur afin de joindre un poste intérieur pour communiquer avec lui ou lui transférer la communication.

Les facilités supplémentaires de l'électronique

• La possibilité de privilégier l'un des postes (secrétariat, accueil...) qui devient terminal prioritaire.

• La faculté d'intervention dans une conversation par le terminal prioritaire.

• Le renvoi des appels sur le poste de votre choix et le filtrage des communications : deux façons de travailler plus tranquillement ou de vous absenter sans risque.

• La réception amplifiée sur haut-parleur qui permet l'information simultanée de votre entourage.

• La faculté de faire participer un collaborateur à la conversation afin d'organiser une conférence à trois.

• La possibilité de savoir quel collaborateur a cherché à vous joindre pendant un appel ou une absence, grâce au clignotement d'un témoin lumineux.

• La numérotation sans décrocher : un gain de temps pour préparer votre conversation.

• Des témoins lumineux indiquant les postes occupés et ceux à rappeler.

.../...

.../...

UN MEILLEUR CONFORT TELEPHONIQUE

- Sous vos yeux, un tableau où sont inscrits tous les numéros d'appel intérieurs.
- Deux ensembles de témoins lumineux, signalant l'état d'occupation de chaque ligne du réseau : libre, en appel, occupé ou en garde.
- Des touches, pour composer rapidement et facilement les numéros d'appel intérieurs ou extérieurs.
- Une sonnerie réglable (timbre et volume).
- La possibilité de supprimer la sonnerie des appels extérieurs, ceux-ci restant cependant signalés par les témoins lumineux.
- Une grande mobilité grâce à un encombrement et un poids réduits.

INTERPHONE ELITE MARK IV

Compact, simple-to-use system incorporating :

- 6 exchange lines and up to 12 extensions.
- Use as both an internal and external phone.
- Full lamp signalling on all extensions.
- Visual display showing numbers dialled, the date and time.
- Hold and transfer facility, enabling you to put calls on hold while you talk to an internal extension and transfer calls between extensions.
- Conference facility to enable 3 extensions to take part in a 3-way discussion.
- Divert facility so that, if you need to be absent, you can transfer calls to a colleague's extension.
- Electronic memory to enable users to store often-used numbers and then dial them at the press of a button.
- Call-timer : a built-in stopwatch for timing the length of calls (thereby keeping costs down!)
- External loudspeaker socket.

Practice

Look at the advertisements for the British and French intercom systems.

1. What is the French for :

hold facility   loudspeaker   extension   lamp signalling   conference facility
exchange lines   transfer facility   button

2. Which of these facilities are offered by the French system and not by the English one?

- interrupt facility (through a priority extension)
- use as an external phone
- amplification through an external loudspeaker
- dialling with the receiver in the cradle
- press-button operation
- hold facility

3. Which facilities are offered by the English system and not by the French one?

Do it yourself

LEAVING AND TAKING MESSAGES

There are four different situations in this activity. Each one involves giving and taking a message. The people are different in each situation.
Choose either A or B . If you are A, read the following instructions. If you are B, **turn to page 51.**

A's instructions

1 Your name is Pat Wilson. You work for Marsh Road Bakeries. (Tel : 54776 4001.) Your company has a utility van — a 1986 BMT 25 — which you would like to trade in for a new one. It has done nearly 50,000 miles and, although it runs well, you think that, if you keep it any longer, you might have expensive repairs in the future. You bought it from Bogdown Motors but that company has changed management and won't give you more than £500 in part exchange. You feel that the van is worth at least £800.
So, you have decided to try Ashburn Motors. You have already visited their showrooms and have decided to buy the Vanguard LR6 if they are willing to give you a good price for your old van. Your contact at Ashburn Motors is Mr Bottomley. Ring him to tell him what you have decided. If he's not there, leave a detailed message.

2 You work for Sound Track Ltd., a small recording studio which specialises in recording cassettes for educational purposes. You work for Mr Shaw who is ill and won't be back until the end of the week. You receive a phone call.

3 Your name is Granger. You are the branch manager of a chain of furniture shops called Wills and Partridge. (Tel : 0659 37865) When you arrived at the shop this morning, there was water coming in through the ceiling and a number of pieces of furniture have been damaged. As this is the first time this has happened you are not sure if you are fully insured against this kind of accident. You are phoning your insurance agent, Mr Bailey, who insured your firm's premises with Mutual Life (policy number : DJ/997/EK/149). If you are insured, you want to know what the procedure is for making a claim. If Mr Bailey isn't in, leave a detailed message. It's 9.05am.

4 You are a "temp" (temporary worker) working for Tasty Treats, a catering firm. It is 5.35pm and everyone else has gone home. You are tidying up the office when the phone rings.

"It's the office. Shall I tell them you're sick?"

6 AFTER THE BEEP

Comprehension

Mr and Mrs Willis are both out at work during the day. For this reason they have got an answerphone so that anyone who calls them can leave a message. They have both just arrived home and are about to play back their messages. Listen and take notes on the messages.

1. One of the callers phones three times. What is the 'story' linking these three messages?
2. Judging from the messages, what do you think Mr Willis's job is?
3. Who is Mr Willis going to call this evening and why?
4. What are Mr and Mrs Willis going to do on Friday evening? Why?
5. Correct these wrongly noted messages :

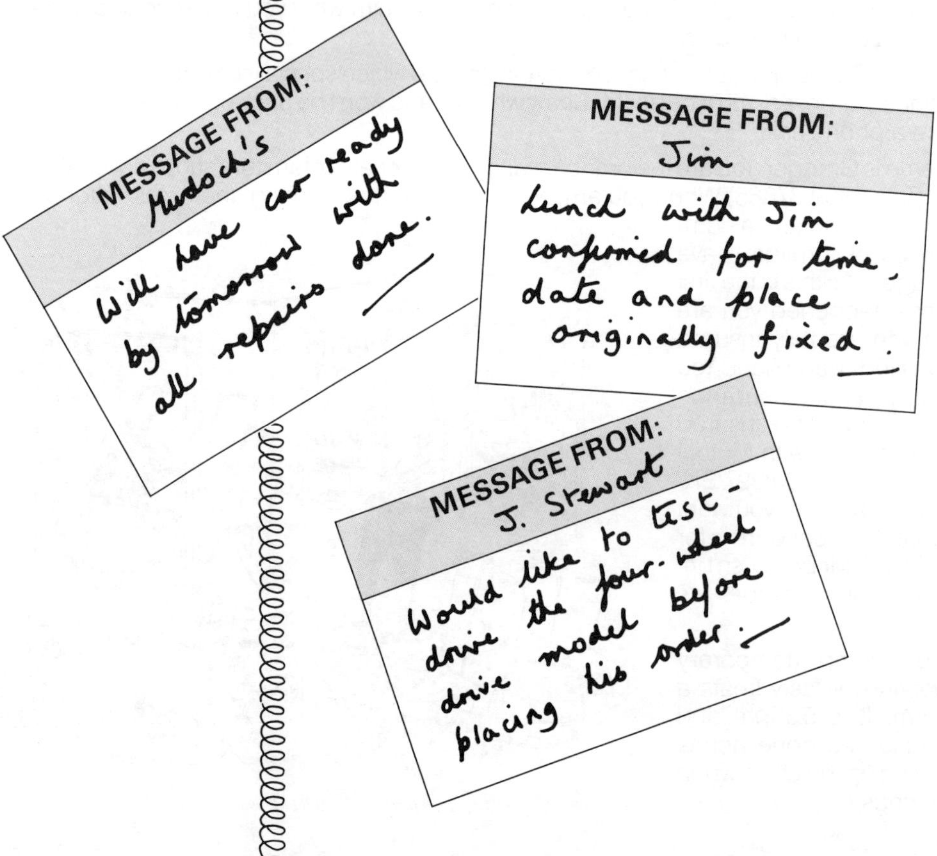

So, you're interested in installing an answering machine, are you?

Well, we've got three models to offer, each for a slightly different purpose.

The **Answermate** is the simplest and cheapest. It simply announces that you are out (or whatever message you care to leave). It does not record your caller's message. Special features :

- Time limit of 3 minutes for the announcement.
- A loud 'beep' tells you that someone is calling. If you are at home with the **Answermate** on and decide to accept a call, simply press the INTERRUPT button when you hear the beep.

.../...

.../...

The **Answerback** records your announcement and plays it to your caller. In addition, it records your caller's message. So, when you get back home, you know who's been trying to get in touch with you. Even if you're at home, you can use it to record messages if you don't want to be disturbed! Its special features include :

- Simple, easy-to-operate recording facility. Just press the RECORD ANNOUNCEMENT button and speak into the built-in microphone. At the end of your announcement, press the END button. That's all you have to do.
- To record messages while you are out, press the AUTOMATIC ANSWER ON button. A green light tells you the answer function is operating.
- A red light tells you that the machine has messages for you to listen to.
- To listen to messages, press the REWIND button. When the tape is rewound, it plays back automatically.
- Incoming messages are limited to 4 minutes.

Answerlux is a very sophisticated model with several interesting features :

- It's set in action by the sound of the human voice. There are no beeps on the announcement tape.
- It is supplied with a remote control device which means you can listen to your messages by calling your number from anywhere in the world.
- An 'Answer only option' allows the machine to operate as a simple answering machine which does not record incoming messages.
- If the message cassette is damaged or has come to the end, this is automatically detected. A flashing sign tells you to CHANGE CASSETTE or REWIND.
- There is no fixed time limit on each incoming message.

Practice

Look at the advertisement for three different answering machines. Assuming that the most sophisticated model incorporates all the special features of the other models, except for the time limits on announcements and messages, complete the following sentences about the Answerlux.

1. Press the RECORD ANNOUNCEMENT button when you..........
2. Press the REWIND button when you........
3. Press the INTERRUPT button if you.....
4. Press the AUTOMATIC ANSWER ON button when you ......
5. Press the END button when you....
6. If you see a flashing sign that says REWIND, it means that.....
7. If you see a green light, it means that...
8. If you see a red light, it means that....
9. If the machine is on "Answer only option" and you hear a loud beep, it means that....
10. If you've left the machine on and have gone abroad on holiday, you can......
11. When you record your announcement, you mustn't say : "Leave a message after the beep" because...
12. You know if your message cassette is damaged because....

Do it yourself

LEAVING RECORDED MESSAGES

A. Announcements

1. You are a travelling salesperson, often away from home. You live alone and you often give your home number to customers as well as to friends. You have just bought an answering machine. Prepare and record the announcement that you would like people to hear. (Invent your English name, number etc.)

2. You are a newly-qualified doctor and, as yet, you don't have a receptionist. Your surgery hours are 9.30 - 12.00 and 4.30 - 6.00. The rest of your time is spent in visiting patients. You have just bought an answering machine. Prepare and record the announcement that you would like people to hear. (Invent your English name, number, etc.)

3. You are a student. You often work in a restaurant in the evenings where you can't take phone calls. You have just bought an answering machine because friends often ring you in the evening when you're at work. Your friends are mostly students too. Prepare and record the announcement that you would like them to hear. (Invent your English name, number, etc.)

B. Messages

1. It's 6.00pm. You are ringing a friend, Jim Highsmith. Jim is out and you are going to leave a message on his answering machine. You have a time limit of 1 1/2 minutes. You have arranged to meet him this evening at 8.00 in front of the Rex cinema. Unfortunately, you are still at work and your boss has asked you to work late. You're not sure when you'll be able to leave. Therefore, you'd prefer to go to the later showing at 10.00. However, since Jim has to be at work early in the morning, you're not sure if he will agree. You want him to ring you at the office when he gets home. Leave your message. (Invent your English name and office number.)

2. It's 10.30am. You're at your office. You've got a terrible toothache and your own dentist is on holiday. A colleague at work has given you the name of another dentist. You want an appointment for today. You ring the dentist and get an answering machine which tells you to leave the necessary details so that the dentist can ring you back early this afternoon. You have a time limit of 1 minute. Leave your message. (Invent your English name and office number.)

3. It is August and a firm which is expecting you to report for a training course on 2nd September has closed for the summer vacation. You are phoning them to say that you will be a couple of days late and to give them your exact time and date of arrival. A recorded announcement tells you to leave a message. Invent your name, your reasons for arriving late, your date and time of arrival, and leave your message. You have a time limit of 2 minutes.

WHEN WOULD IT BE CONVENIENT ?

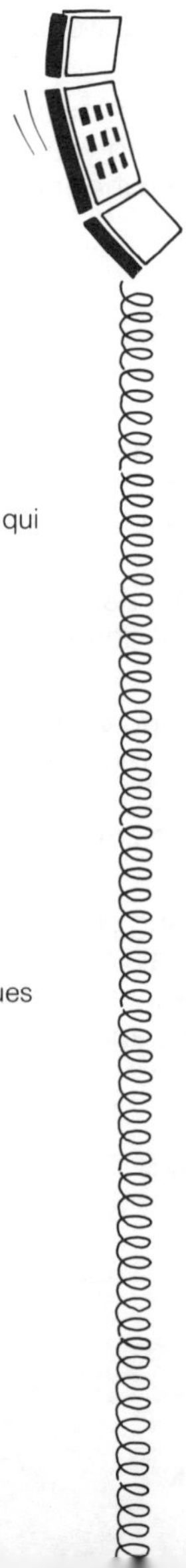

Helen Cook is a housewife. It's 11.00am and she's just poured herself a cup of coffee when the phone rings. Listen to the conversation and fill in the blanks.

HELEN : Brighton 4263.

SUE : Hello, is that Mrs Cook?

HELEN : Speaking.

SUE : Good morning, Mrs Cook. How are you today?

HELEN : Er...fine, thank you. ① ________________________________ ?

SUE : My name's Sue. We don't know each other but I'm calling on behalf of a company I'm sure you've heard of. ② ________________ our advertisements in the local press for Albion Double Glazing.

HELEN : Sorry, what was that?

SUE : Albion Double Glazing. We're the biggest suppliers of energy-saving installations in the region. And the reason I'm ringing you is just to ③ ________________ about your house and the way you try to keep it warm in winter. Do you have central heating, Mrs Cook?

HELEN : Er...yes, we do.

SUE : Gas or electric?

HELEN : Electric.

SUE : Uh huh. So, I ④ ________________ that with the winters

① Puis-je demander qui est à l'appareil

② Vous avez dû voir

③ vous poser quelques questions

④ suppose

we've been having, that must work out pretty expensive. ⑤ ______________________, Mrs Cook, how much your last heating bill came to ?

HELEN : I've really no idea, but my husband nearly had a heart attack when he signed the cheque.

SUE : Well yes, I'm not surprised. And ⑥ ______________ he might be interested in saving at least 10% on the bill — perhaps more ?

HELEN : Why yes, of course he would.

SUE : And you, Mrs Cook. ⑦ ____________________ that some of the rooms in the house are a bit cold in the winter even with the central heating on?

HELEN : Well, yes, now you mention it, there's a room that faces north. In fact ⑧ ______________________ a bigger radiator in there. When there's a wind in that direction, the window's covered in ice in the morning.

SUE : I see. Yes. Well, you see, that's where double glazing is so useful. It keeps the cold air out, prevents draughts, stops condensation and keeps all the warm air in. And the whole house is so much more comfortable.

HELEN : Well, ⑨ ______________________. But I'd have to ask my husband first.

SUE : Of course. ⑩ ________________________ when he comes back home from work ?

HELEN : About 6. Between 6 and 6.30.

SUE : Right. Well look, Mrs Cook, let me make a suggestion. Our representative will be in your area shortly. ⑪ ____________ ____________ have a look at the problem and give you some advice ?

HELEN : Well, er...I'd like to have time to think about it.

SUE : Naturally, but it would be a good idea to talk about your needs with one of our technicians, ⑫ ______________ ? And don't worry, Mrs Cook, a visit ⑬ ________________

HELEN : No, I suppose not.

SUE : ⑭ ________________________________ at 7 o'clock?

HELEN : Well, that might be a little early. We usually have dinner about then.

SUE : O.K., ⑮ __________, ⑯ ____________

HELEN : Er...well.... ⑰ __________________________ ?

SUE : Right. That's fine. Well, it's been nice talking to you. Goodbye, Mrs Cook. Have a nice day.

HELEN : Thank you. Goodbye.

⑤ Cela vous dérangerait-il de me dire
⑥ ne pensez-vous pas (que)
⑦ Ne trouvez-vous pas
⑧ nous pensons installer
⑨ ça a l'air intéressant
⑩ Puis-je vous demanmander
⑪ Si on lui demandait de passer
⑫ n'est-ce pas
⑬ ne vous engage à rien
⑭ D'accord pour demain soir
⑮ comme vous voulez
⑯ c'est à vous de décider
⑰ Et 19.45

PRESTEL

Prestel is the trademark of British Telecom's public viewdata service and allows you to get instant access to information and services. It links your telephone line to your microcomputer or your television so that this information can then be called up over the ordinary telephone line and displayed on the screen.
You can see what's on at the theatre or get the latest sports results, consult travel timetables, book a room in a hotel or look for a house to buy from estate agents' lists. There are over 1,000 Information Providers and more than 250,000 pages of information.
Are you fed up with queueing up in supermarkets? Why not go teleshopping? You can browse through the electronic catalogues page by page and then place your order by completing response frames on the screen. You simply supply your credit card number and the goods will arrive on your doorstep — all without moving from your armchair.
You can connect your computer to something called Homelink which enables you to consult banks directly to ask about interest rates, transfer funds, or perhaps apply for a loan. You can get financial information such as Stock Exchange prices from Citiservice. You can send messages instantaneously to companies or individuals that use the Electronic Mailbox, and get a reply back straight away. There is also a telex service which is very cheap. You don't need a telex terminal or telex line : you just dial into Prestel, log on with a confidential password and then compose your telex which is then transmitted over the telex network. A telex costs about £1 for a hundred words in the U.K., £3 to North America and £4 to the rest of the world. You can also receive telexes free of charge.
As a Prestel subscriber, you pay a quarterly standing charge plus a time charge which applies when a connection to Prestel is made during a standard rate period. You pay by the minute. Most of the information pages are free, but some specialist Information Providers have a price per page which is displayed on the screen. There are also the telephone costs which are, in most cases, at local call rates and which are included on the normal telephone bill.

Practice

1. Using the information in the text, fill in the blanks in the following passage, so that you obtain a description of what Prestel is. The blanks do not correspond to the length of the words that fill them.

Prestel enables you to gain .... to both .... and .... What it does basically is to .... your telephone line to your .... or your .... which means that you can .... this information at any time of the day or night and see .... If you decide to .... to Prestel, you will have to pay for .... to the network, but most of the .... are free.

2. Which of the following Prestel services are not mentioned in the text ? Are there any services mentioned in the text which are not on the list?

hotel reservations — weather forecasts — train and ferry timetables — "where to eat" guides
sports results — consumer advice — home banking — theatre bookings

3. Fill in the table below to show how, Prestel is paid for :

Equipment or service	How paid for/fee
Prestel subscription	....
Connection to Prestel network	....
Information pages	....
Telephone call charges	....
Telex	....

Do it yourself

MAKING AN APPOINTMENT

A works in the sales department of a large firm producing ready-to-wear clothes. He/she is phoning B, the factory manager of a textile company, to make an appointment in order to see their new range of textiles. Both A and B are extremely busy people. A is closely involved with his/her children's school, and B is a local councillor.
Choose your part (A or B). If you are A, read the following instructions. If you are B, turn to page 52 for your instructions.

A's instructions

It's Friday afternoon and you are phoning **B** to fix an appointment for next week. You want to see their new collection of textiles at their factory. Look at your diary and see what your engagements are for next week. Fix an appointment and write it in your diary.

	Mon	Tues	Wed	Thurs	Fri	Sat
8			Flight to			
(9)	View new		Copenhagen			
10	TV commercial					
11	at advertising	Lunch Mr. Adams				
12	agency.	at Funfabrik				
13						
14				back from		Collect
(15)	collect leaflets			Copenhagen		Susan.
16	+ display stands					
17	from printers					
18					Swimming	
(19)	children's				Committee	
20	school meeting				meeting	
21						

8 THERE'S SOMETHING WRONG

Comprehension

Listen to Conversation 1. Mr Weston has just received a gas bill which he thinks is too high. He's phoning the local Gas Board.

1. What is Mr Weston's account number?
2. How much is the bill for?
3. Why does Mr Weston think the bill is so high?
4. How many expressions can you remember that Mr Weston used to state his dissatisfaction and suggest that something was wrong? Make a list of the expressions.
5. How would you describe Mr Weston's tone and attitude?

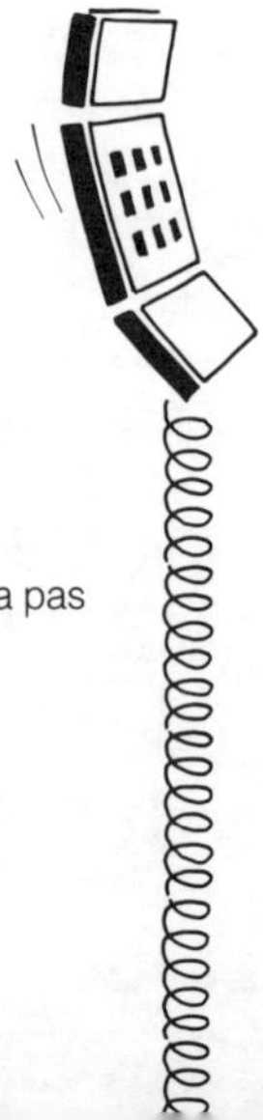

Listen to Conversation 2. Roland Wells is a film director on location making a new Western. It is early morning and he's setting up the cameras for a particularly difficult sequence. He's talking to various technicians over his cellphone. He's already in a bad mood. Fill in the blanks in the conversation.

ROLAND : O.K. Is camera 3 in position?

MAN 1 : No. We'll need about another 30 minutes.

ROLAND : Why? ① ______________ ?

MAN 1 : We've got a problem with the cable. But it's O.K. Nothing serious.

① Qu'est-ce qui ne va pas

② Je commence à en avoir marre

③ Il est temps

④ J'en ai assez

⑤ Et pourquoi pas, bon Dieu ?

⑥ tu ne peux pas te dépêcher ?

⑦ C'est le bouquet

ROLAND : Fine.

WOMAN : Roland? There's no sign of Glenda Frazer yet. She was supposed to be ready in costume half an hour ago.

ROLAND : Oh God ! ② ____________________ with her attitude ! Go and find her and tell her that if she's not here in ten minutes, I'll find another heroine. ③ ____________________ she realised she's not the centre of the universe. It's the third time this has happened this week. ④ ____________________ of her playing games !

WOMAN : All right, Roland.

ROLAND : Camera 1. Ready?

MAN 2 : Er..no. We've got a problem here. We've..er...run out of film.

ROLAND : What do you mean you've run out of film?

MAN 2 : What I said.

ROLAND : Why am I surrounded by imbeciles?

MAN 2 : I don't know, Roland. But don't worry we'll be ready by 6.

ROLAND : You'd better be. What about the lighting. Fred? Fred? Come in, Fred.

MAN 3 : This is Fred, Roland. Sorry, we haven't finished setting up the lights yet.

ROLAND : What? ⑤ ____________________ ?

MAN 3 : We've had a few problems.

ROLAND : Well, ⑥ ____________________. This is a very difficult scene.

MAN 3 : I know. That's why I want to get it right.

WOMAN : Hello, Roland. Apparently, Glenda is still at her hotel. She's refusing to leave without her breakfast, and the hotel won't serve breakfast at this time of the morning.

ROLAND : Oh no ! ⑦ ____________________ !
I resign !

Comprehension

Listen to Conversations 3 and 4. In the first conversation, Gordon Phillips is with a client in a restaurant. In the second, he is in his car driving to another appointment after lunch.

1. How many expressions for making an apology did you hear in the conversations ? Which of these expressions could be called 'formal', and which 'informal' ?

2. How many expressions did you hear that can be used by someone who has just received an apology and wants to say that "It isn't a problem"?

CELLPHONES

Practice

1. Read the advertisement for Cellphones, adapted from a British Telecom ad. Make a sentence to explain each of the following expressions :

a sun roof — to call base — to run out (of money) — two-digit dialling
pre-programmed numbers — "hands-free" facility — to put to good use

2. According to the advertisement, what are the advantages of having a carphone?

CCC Practice

Who do you think each of the people in the illustration is speaking to?

Do it yourself

COMPLAINING AND APOLOGISING

A is phoning a department store to complain about something. B is the manager of the complaints department.
Choose your part (A or B). If you are A, read the following instructions. If you are B, turn to page 52.

A's instructions

You ordered two folding chairs from a department store two weeks ago. They were priced at £15 each. The sales assistant told you that they would be delivered within a week and that you could pay 'cash on delivery'. The assistant didn't mention anything about a delivery charge. The chairs have just arrived. Not only are they late but the bill was for £45 ! You have paid the delivery man because otherwise the chairs would be taken back to the store, but you are furious. You are sure the store has made a mistake somewhere. You want to know why the bill was for £45 instead of £30, and you want £15 back ! Your name is J.Weston. The order N° is 633 and the reference number of the chairs : CH/159X. You have just rung the store and are waiting for the complaints department manager to answer.

9 AT YOUR SERVICE

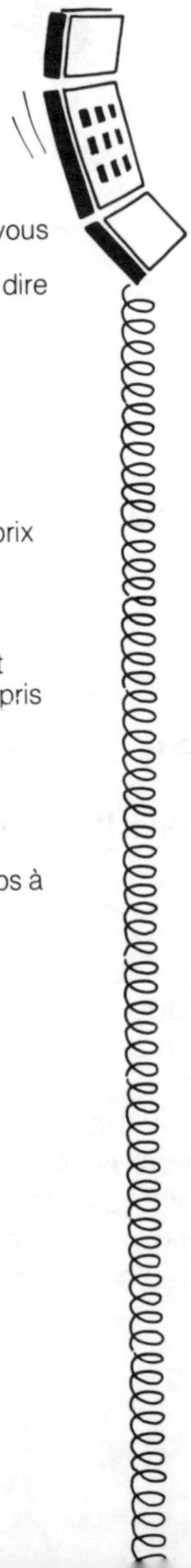

Listen to Conversation 1. A woman is phoning the Lincoln Hotel for information. Fill in the blanks as you listen.

RECEPTION : Lincoln Hotel. ① ______________________ ?

WOMAN : Yes please. ② ______________________________ ______________ for a double room, please?

RECEPTION : Certainly, madam. With or without a private bathroom?

WOMAN : Well, it depends. ③ ______________________________ ____ ?

RECEPTION : Yes, of course. With bath it's £75 and without, £60.

WOMAN : ④ __________________________ in that?

RECEPTION : No, madam. Breakfast is extra, and the price depends on whether it's a Continental breakfast or English style.

WOMAN : I see. Well, thank you very much. ⑤ ____________________ do I need to book?

RECEPTION : Well, I'm afraid we're fully booked until the end of August, madam.

WOMAN : No, this would be for September.

RECEPTION : Well, the sooner the better. ⑥ __________ at least ⑦ __________________________ if possible.

WOMAN : Right. Thank you.

RECEPTION : ⑧ ____________ , madam. Goodbye.

WOMAN : Goodbye.

① Que puis-je pour vous
② Pourriez-vous me dire le prix
③ Pouvez-vous me donner les deux prix
④ Est-ce que le petit déjeuner est compris
⑤ Combien de temps à l'avance
⑥ Disons
⑦ trois semaines à l'avance
⑧ Je vous en prie

Comprehension

Listen to Conversation 2. Mr Hargreaves is a guest at the Lincoln Hotel. He's phoning reception for information. Take notes as you listen.

1. There's a brochure on Mr Hargreaves' desk. What does it say about :
- The London-by-night tour?
- The cabaret show?

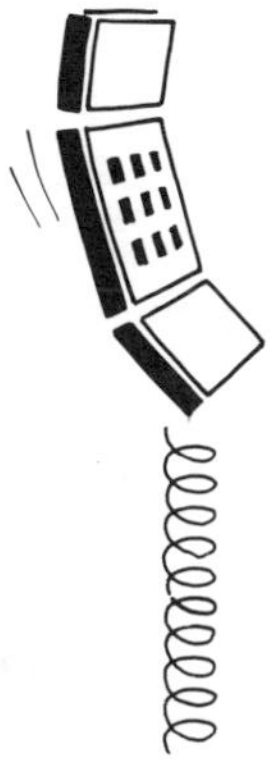

Comprehension

Listen to Conversation 3. A woman is phoning the Lincoln Hotel for information. Take notes as you listen.

1. What exactly is the receptionist going to send the woman?
2. Write down the woman's name and address.
3. What words are used in the conversation to express the following ideas :
- I want some information about...
- Does it show clearly...
- I'll send one off today.

Listen to Conversation 4. A man is phoning the Lincoln Hotel from Paris. As you listen, fill in the blanks.

RECEPTION : Reception, Lincoln Hotel. Can I help you?

MAN : Hello. I'm ringing from Paris. My name is Watkins and I have a ① __________ for Sunday night. Train plus hotel scheme from Paris.

RECEPTION : Mr Watkins....Yes, sir. ② ____________________ __________, arriving Sunday. 3 nights.

MAN : Yes, well, ③ ____________________ . I may want to stay on an extra night. Is there any problem?

RECEPTION : Just one moment sir......No, that would be fine. But if you do stay on, it would be ④ ____________________ not the ⑤ ______________ .

MAN : Oh, I see. ⑥ ______________________________ ?

RECEPTION : I believe it's about double the reduced rate, sir ⑦ ______________________________ the exact figure?

MAN : No. No,what interests me is an extra day at the reduced rate. Isn't that possible?

RECEPTION : ⑧ ____________________ , sir. Not unless you change your booking in Paris.

MAN : Right. Well, I'd better do that then. Thank you anyway.

RECEPTION : ⑨ ____________________ , sir. Goodbye.

MAN : Goodbye.

① réservation
② Chambre simple avec douche
③ justement
④ plein tarif
⑤ tarif réduit
⑥ Combien ça serait en plus
⑦ Voulez-vous que je vous donne
⑧ J'ai peur que non
⑨ Je vous en prie

GUIDELINES

British Telecom provides a number of information and entertainment services that you can get simply by dialling the appropriate number. The charge is the same as for an ordinary phone call. The Guidelines vary from area to area. The ones on this page are for the Greater London area.

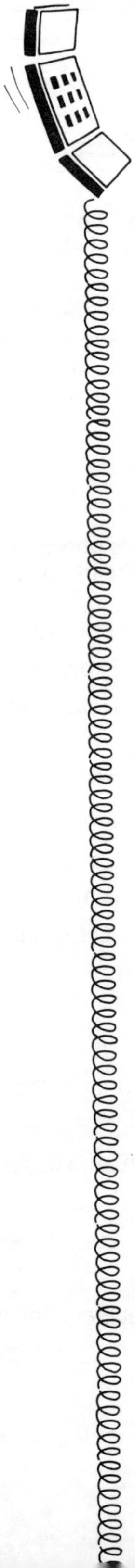

Practice

Look at the Guideline descriptions on this page and listen to the twelve extracts on tape. Which extract fits which Guideline? Give reasons for your choice.

A F.T. Cityline

For business news
and frequently updated F.T. Index.
Dial 01-246 8026.

B Cricketline

Find out the current state of play,
8am - 7pm during major matches.
Dial 154.

C Timeline

Keep track of the right time.
Dial 123.

D William Hill Raceline

Find out if you're on course
for a big win.
For up-to-the-minute information.
Dial 168.

E Sportsline

Get the latest sports round-up.
Dial 01-246 8020.

F Leisureline

Daily selection of events
in and around London.
In English 01-246 8041.
In French 01-246 8043.
In German 01-246 8045.

G Carebear Bedtime Storyline

Are you sitting comfortably?
Then we'll begin.
From 6pm each evening.
Dial 01-246 8000.

H Discline

Chart your favourite discs.
Dial 160.

I **Traveline**

See how your road, rail, air or sea route is affected. Dial 01-246 8021.

K **Capital Radioline**

Tune into your favourite programmes. Dial 01-246 8024.

J **Newsline**

News bulletin updated hourly. Dial 01-246 8080.

L **Weatherline**

For what the weather will, won't or might do in London. Dial 01-246 8091.

Do it yourself

ASKING FOR AND GIVING INFORMATION

A is phoning to cancel a coach tour from London to Oxford. B works for the travel agency who booked the tour.
Choose your part (A or B). If you are A, read the following instructions. If you are B, turn to page 53.

A's instructions

You and a couple of friends are on holiday in England and have booked a coach tour from London to Oxford tomorrow. (Below is a description of the tour you have booked. You will need to describe it briefly when making your phone call as there may be more than one Oxford excursion.) Unfortunately, one of your friends has gastroenteritis and you have therefore decided to cancel the tour. You are phoning Roy Eames Travel Agency to cancel and to get your money back. If it is not possible to get your money back, you will book a similar tour instead. If you have to book a similar tour, you will need to know :
• how much it costs • what it includes • the dates • the place of departure

OXFORD EXCURSION

Departing from Warwick Avenue at 8.00am, we go by way of Henley-on-Thames, cross the picturesque Chiltern Hills and arrive in Oxford at 10.30 after a short break for morning coffee. We visit one of the principal colleges and have time to shop in the pleasant old part of the town before meeting up for lunch at one of the city's top quality restaurants. In the afternoon there will be an opportunity to see a play performed at the famous Playhouse Theatre. Return to London for 6.00pm.

Tour N66 - with lunch
Adult : £15.50 Child : £9.00

Tour N67 - without lunch
Adult : £10.50 Child : £4.50

Departure : 66, Warwick Avenue. 8.00am

REVISION

Comprehension

Listen to the 8 extracts of telephone conversations.

1. For each of the extracts, say as much as you can about the reason for the phone call.
2. Use your imagination and, for each conversation, complete the sentence that the final speaker has started.

Vocabulary

Use words or expressions from the list below to complete the following sentences. (In the case of a verb, put it into the correct tense.)

hook alarm call slot beep pips rewind
put through interference standing charge
directory digit hold on

1. If you want to find someone's number, you can look it up in the ________ .
2. In a public call box, you have to put your coins in the ________ .
3. When you hear the ______ , it means you've got to put more money in.
4. When the switchboard operator in a company is trying to connect you to the extension you want, he or she will probably say : "I'm ________ you ________ ."
5. When you want a caller to wait while you transfer him or her to another extension, you might say : "________ , please."
6. When you are phoning long distance, there is sometimes a lot of ________ on the line.
7. When you want to be woken up early in the morning, you ask for an ________ .
8. Some phones allow you to dial without taking the receiver off the ________ .
9. You usually have to wait for the ______ before leaving a message on an answering machine.
10. If you want to go back to the beginning of a tape or cassette, the button you press is called "________".
11. The fixed sum that you pay at regular intervals for a service like Prestel is called the ________ .
12. A ______ is another word for a single number or figure.

Matching

Match each "dialogue extract" (1-10) to the appropriate situation description (A-J).

1. "Here it is, sir, on the counter. Just put your money in the slot and dial the number."
2. "There's nothing to worry about. These things often fade out when there's interference. We've just gone past some overhead cables."
3. "The outside lines are on this side. And these lamps tell you which extensions are busy at the moment."
4. "No, it won't work from the other end of the garden. The range is limited."
5. "No, I didn't actually see it happen. How long will it take before the ambulance gets here?"
6. "Roadworks in progress on the northbound carriageway are causing severe delays."
7. "Oh no! I've been cut off! Have you got any more 10p coins?"
8. "Why is it doing that? I asked it for departure times of trains from London Bridge to Charing Cross."
9. "He's not in his office, but I think I know where to find him. Just hold the line, and I'll try another extension."
10. "If you want to leave a message, you can do so after the beep."

A. Your friend is trying to find out train times on your Prestel and has done something wrong.
B. You are connected to an answering machine.
C. Someone is showing you how a switchboard works.
D. You have asked for a phone in a restaurant where they have a small desktop Payphone.
E. You are having a slight problem with a cordless telephone.
F. There's a drop in sound quality on the Cellphone in your car.
G. You haven't put enough money in the slot.
H. You are phoning an emergency service.
I. The operator is trying to put you through to the person you want to speak to.
J. You've phoned a Guideline service for information.

Invention

Using the "flow-chart", invent the conversation. At the end of the conversation, write the message.

David Marks is in New York. He's calling Elizabeth North at her office in London. She works for General Electronics. David and Elizabeth are due to have a meeting the day after tomorrow (Friday) in Paris but David won't be able to leave New York until Sunday because....(you invent the reason). Elizabeth will therefore have to reschedule her flight and hotel reservation if she is still free. If she isn't free, they will have to come to a different arrangement.

David	Elizabeth's company
	Switchboard : Answer
Ask for Elizabeth.	
	Ask caller to wait. Inform caller that line is engaged.
Ask to wait.	
	Agree. (After few seconds) inform caller that you are connecting him.
Thank switchboard.	
	Secretary : Answer.
Ask if the person answering is Elizabeth North.	
	Inform caller that Elizabeth North has left.
Ask for Elizabeth's home number.	
	Inform caller that giving home numbers isn't allowed. Ask for his identity.
Give identity. Explain urgency.	
	Offer to take a message.
Give message.	
	Explain that Elizabeth North will receive message tomorrow morning.
Thank and sign off.	
	Sign off.

ANNEXES

PART B

UNIT 2

B's instructions

1. You have just witnessed an accident. A car has had a head-on collision with a lorry. No one is hurt. You have just rung the emergency services and have asked for the police. You are waiting for them to answer. The number of the phone box you're calling from is 0473 8091. The plan below tells you where you are and where the accident took place.

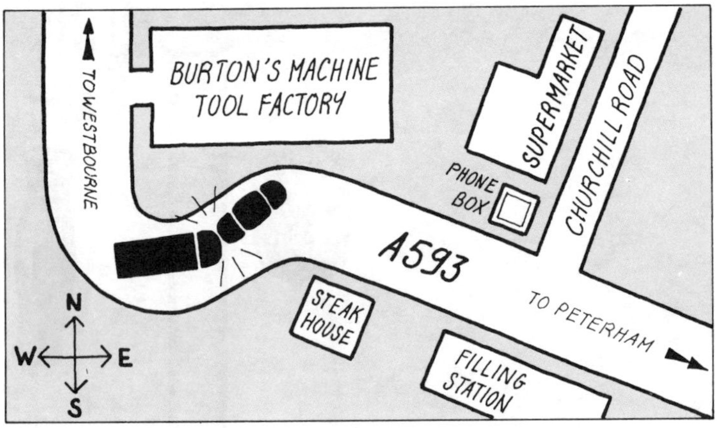

2. You are the switchboard operator for the Fire Brigade emergency service. The phone has just rung. Answer it and say : "Fire Brigade. Can I help you?" In order to send help to anyone, you need the caller's name, number, location and the location of the emergency.

3. You were walking along the sea front in Seasalter when you suddenly noticed two emergency flares (luminous distress signals) offshore. You have run to the nearest phone box and have called the emergency services. You have asked for the coastguard. The number of the phone box is 1566 00134. Your location and the approximate location of the emergency flares are shown on the map below.

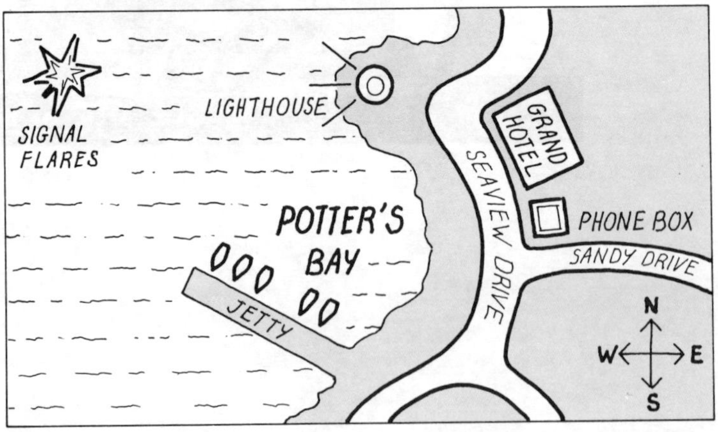

4. You are the switchboard operator for the police emergency service. It's late at night and the phone has just rung. Answer it and say : "Police. Can I help you?". In order to send help to anyone, you need the caller's name, number, location and the location of the emergency. If a crime is involved, get as many details as you can from the witness. If necessary, you can contact the ambulance service yourself.

UNIT 3

B's instructions

You live at 30, Barton Close. You have given your address to a friend who you have invited to your house after his/her English class at the language school (college). Your friend rings you. Using the map below, give him/her precise directions, indicating any landmarks that you think will help him/her to find his/her way.

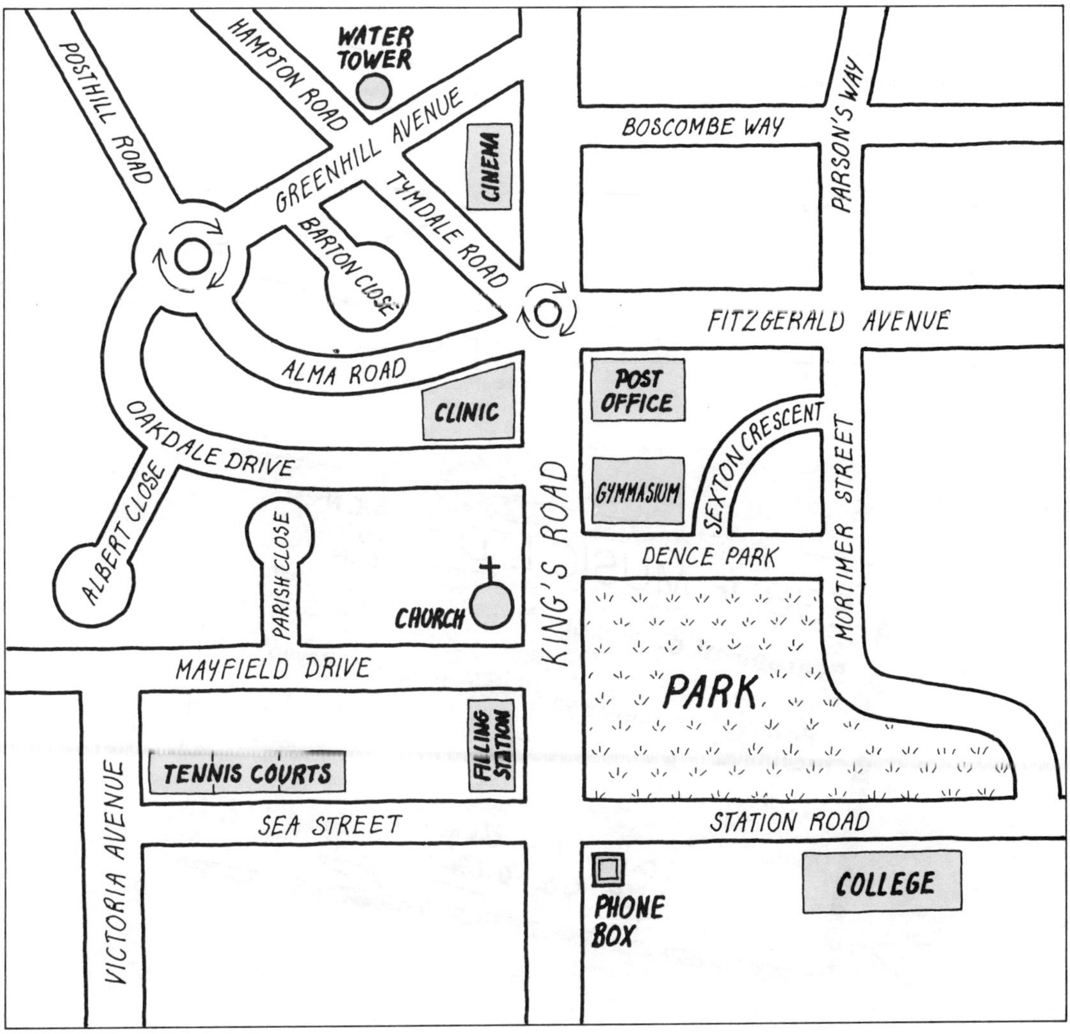

UNIT 4

B's instructions

You work in the Royalties Department of EGBDF Music Ltd. The manager, Mr Callan is out at the moment. You receive a phone call. Work out what you will say from the chart below and a copy of the royalty statement which you find in the dossier.

Lift the receiver and acknowledge.

Ask who is calling.

Say that Mr Callan is out and offer to help instead.

Offer to look in the dossier and check.

Give answers from the statement of account.

Ring off.

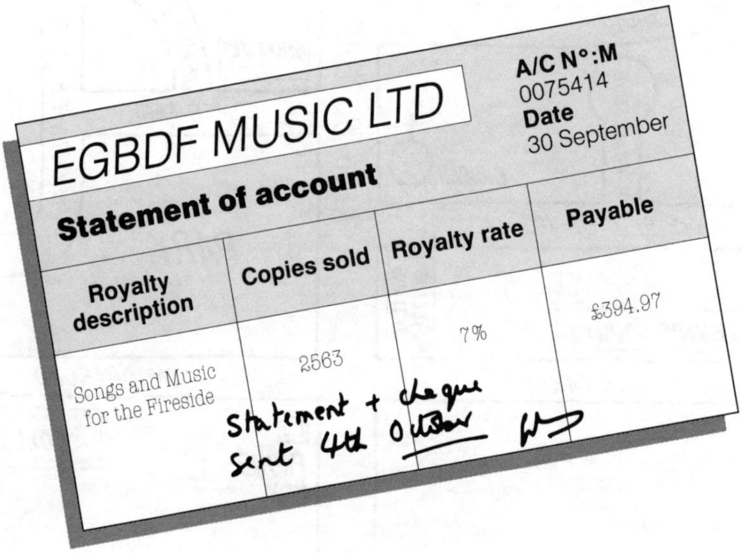

UNIT 5

B's instructions

1. You work at Ashburn Motors, a company that buys and sells new and second-hand vehicles. Your boss, Mr Bottomley is with an important customer at the moment and you can't disturb him. You receive a phone call from a potential customer.

2. Your name is Francis/Frances* Makin. You work for Desktop Press, a publisher of educational material. (Tel. 9855 90302). You have just produced a new commercial English course for foreign students called *Mind Your Own Business*. The course consists of a text book and 2 cassettes and is advertised in your catalogue. The book is already available but unfortunately, Sound Track Ltd, the studio where the cassettes were recorded two months ago, have still not sent you the master tapes for duplication. Teachers who have bought the course are phoning you all the time to know when the cassettes will be available. If they aren't available very soon, you risk losing a lot of business. You are ringing Mr Shaw of Sound Track Ltd, to find out why the delay has occurred and when the tapes will be delivered. You are extremely annoyed. If Mr Shaw is out, leave a detailed message.

3. You are a secretary. You have been working for Bailey's Insurance Brokers for the past ten days. As yet, you know very little about the business. It is 9.05am and Mr Bailey has not arrived yet.

4. Your name is Mr/Ms James, the local representative of a Japanese firm, Bonzai Computers. (Tel: 0455 67675). You have just received their latest product, a miniature computer called "Keyman 25", and you want to launch it at a reception on Thursday 4th of next month at the Norfolk Conference Rooms, 65 Charles Street, Watford, at 7.00pm. You will be inviting about 50 people — journalists and potential customers — and want a caterer to provide and serve a buffet supper. You went to a reception last month given by Ilford Electronics and you remember that the caterer was called Tasty Treats. You would like exactly the same sort of buffet as Ilford Electronics provided. You have just found Tasty Treats' number in the phone book. It's late in the afternoon but you decide to ring them. If you can't get the right person, leave a detailed message.

*"Francis" is a man's first name. "Frances" is for a woman.

UNIT 7

B's instructions

You are the production manager of a textile manufacturing company and also a local councillor. It's Friday afternoon. You are in your office when the phone rings. You've got your diary in front of you. It shows you what your engagements are for next week. Using the information in the diary, fix an appointment to meet your caller next week.

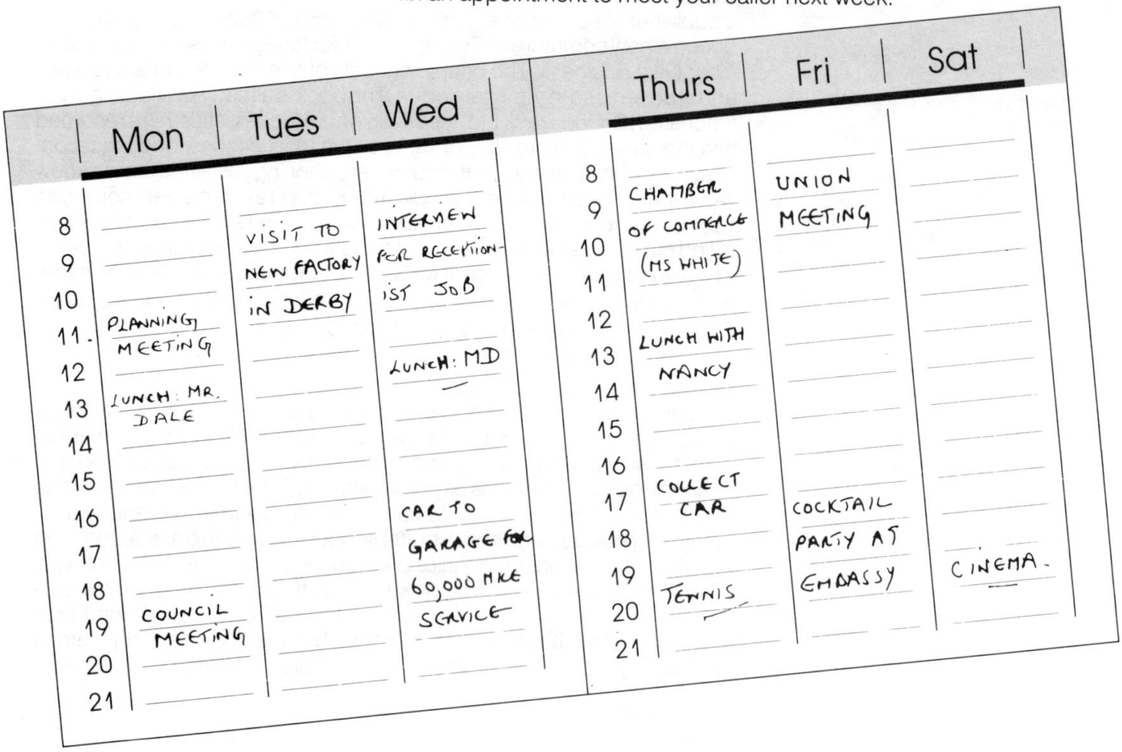

UNIT 8

B's instructions

You are the manager of the complaints department at a large department store. You have been receiving a lot of complaints recently from customers who have had goods delivered and have not realised that there is a delivery charge of £15 on every separate order. You have traced this back to the fact that many of the temporary staff you have taken on recently do not know about delivery charges. You have made sure that they know now ! In front of you is a computer with a complete listing of customer orders, bills etc. You can consult this very easily. In order to do so, you need the customer's name, the order number and the reference number of the item(s) ordered. The computer then tells you the amount of the bill. You are free to do whatever you like in order to keep good customer relations. You can ask for a credit note to be issued or even refund money if you think it's necessary. But you'd rather not do this if a customer can be pacified by an apology.

The phone has just rung in your office. Answer it.

When you consult your computer, it will show the bill as being:

£30 + £15 delivery charge = £45

UNIT 9

B's instructions

You work at Roy Eames Travel Agency. You receive a phone call from a customer who wishes to cancel a tour. There is normally a 40% cancellation fee unless another tour is booked. You have a lot of London-Oxford excursions tomorrow and, in order to make a reservation or cancellation, you need the reference number of the tour and a brief description of it. Next week, there is no tour to Oxford, but there is a special tour to Norwich which you would like to fill. Below is an extract from your brochure describing the tour.

THE CITY OF NORWICH

Norwich is indeed a great city: a city of architecture — the heritage of a thousand years of history; a city of learning with its famous university; a city of music; a city of drama; a city of art with its important schools of painting; a city of traditional crafts and industry; bell-making, weaving, shoemaking, textiles, and many more.

Leaving from Belgrave Square at 7.00am we drive through pleasant open roads, stopping on the way for refreshments and arriving in Norwich at 11.00am. Time to visit the historic cathedral and then Elm Hill with its pleasant cobbled streets and fine old mediaeval buildings. After lunch at the White Horse Inn where touring Elizabethan musicians played, spend the afternoon in the Folk Museum, in Stranger's Hall (home of Norwich's mayors), or in Norwich Castle, and end the day shopping in the famous open market. Back in London for 8.30pm.

Tour N°83 - with lunch and guided tour
Adult: £25.65 Child: £15.75

Tour N°84 - without lunch or guided tour
Adult: £16.75 Child: £8.50

TAPESCRIPTS

UNIT 2

Conversation 1

OPERATOR : McCullough and Bride. Can I help you?

MAN : Good morning, could you put me through to Mr. "Teelair" please?

OPERATOR : Mr. Dealer ? I'm afraid there's no one of that name who works here. Are you sure about the name?

MAN : Er...yes. I met him at the trade fair in Birmingham two weeks ago. He gave me his card and we arranged...

OPERATOR : What did you say his name was?

MAN : Mr "Teelair". He works in the export department.

OPERATOR : I don't know that name. There's Mr Foster, Mr Burton, Mr Tyler, Mr Blake....

MAN : Ah ! Mr Tyler — yes, that's him. I'm sorry. It's my pronunciation.

OPERATOR : Mr Tyler. Right. I'll put you through now.

....

OPERATOR : Hello. I'm sorry, the line's engaged. Would you like to hold on or would you rather ring back later ?

MAN : Er...no, I'd like to leave a message, please. Could you tell Mr Tyler that Monsieur Aimé phoned from France and ask him to phone me as soon as he can ?

OPERATOR : Certainly. How do you spell your name, please?

MAN : Er... *(il épèle à la française)* A *(ah)*...I *(eee)*...M.....E *(é)*

OPERATOR : O.K. then, Mr.....Rema. I'll give him your message.

MAN : Er...yes.....

OPERATOR : Goodbye.

MAN : Goodbye. ....Thank you.

UNIT 4

Conversation 1

MAN : 1.....9.....2....

OPERATOR : Directory Enquiries. Which town?

MAN : Oh..er....hello..er...I'm not sure.

OPERATOR : Well, I can't give you a number unless I know the town.

MAN : Yes, sure, I know that. It's someone I know or rather, met in Scotland. He lives in the Aberdeen area.

OPERATOR : Aberdeen, then. What name was it?

MAN : Well, it's not really in Aberdeen. It's somewhere near Aberdeen, but I've forgotten the name of the place. It's something like Kirkwall. Does that mean anything to you?

OPERATOR : No. But give me the name and I'll look up the Aberdeen area.

MAN : Well the name is Ian McIntyre...or perhaps McIntosh.

OPERATOR : You don't know ?!?

MAN : Well, you could look under McIntyre. In Aberdeen.

OPERATOR : Is it M-C or M-A-C ?

MAN : I'm afraid I don't know. I'm sorry to be so vague.

OPERATOR : I'll look under both.

MAN : Thank you.

OPERATOR : There's a McIntyre in Torry Street.

MAN : No. This person lives in Ruthrieston Road.

OPERATOR : Ah! Well, why didn't you say so? How do you spell that?

MAN : R-U-T-H-R-I-E-S-T-O-N

OPERATOR : I'll try M-A-C for McIntyre. No, there's no McIntyre at that address. What was that town you mentioned?

MAN : Er...Kirkwall, I think.

OPERATOR : I'll see if there's anywhere like that in the Aberdeen district. There's a place called Kingswells. Does that ring a bell?

MAN : Yes, that's it ! Kingswells. It's on the A944 as you drive out of Aberdeen.

OPERATOR : So, we know the name isn't McIntyre, and we know the place is Kingswells. I'll look under McIntosh. M-C I suppose. Here we are. McIntosh I.,

19, Ruthrieston Road, Kingswells. The number's 34899.

MAN : 34899. Wonderful. And could you tell me the area code?

OPERATOR : 0244.

MAN : Thank you. Thank you very much. Sorry to have put you to so much trouble.

OPERATOR : That's quite all right. Goodbye.

UNIT 5

Conversation 1

OPERATOR : Manchester Exhibition Centre. Good afternoon.

MAN : Could I speak to the Director, please?

OPERATOR : I'm afraid he's out at the moment, and his secretary's at lunch. Can I help you at all?

MAN : Well, you wrote and asked us for an estimate for the installation of a PMBX switchboard. We sent you the estimate over a month ago, and we haven't heard from you since. We're a bit surprised because we understood at the time it was fairly urgent. So, I was wondering if Mr Gordon has had the time to study our proposal, because we too have to plan our work schedule.

OPERATOR : Right. I see. Could I have your name please, sir ? And your company?

MAN : It's Digital Electronics, and my name's Jeffrey Paxton. Would you ask Mr Gordon to ring me back as soon as possible, please?

OPERATOR : Yes, sir.

MAN : He's got our number. And he can reach me on extension 54.

OPERATOR : Right, sir. I'll see he gets the message.

MAN : Thank you. Goodbye.

OPERATOR : Goodbye.

Conversation 2

OPERATOR : Manchester Exhibition Centre. Good afternoon. Can I help you?

WOMAN : Yes. I'm phoning about hiring floor space for the Textile Machinery Exhibition in April. Could you tell me how much it would be for 50 square metres?

OPERATOR : I'm sorry, I can't tell you offhand. It's really a matter for the Stand Hire section, and they're at lunch now.

WOMAN : Could you leave a message and ask them to ring me back.

OPERATOR : Certainly. Your name is.....

WOMAN : Jane Bauman.

OPERATOR : Bowman?

WOMAN : No, Bauman. B-A-U-M-A-N.

OPERATOR : And your telephone number?

WOMAN : 3875929

OPERATOR : Any particular time suit you Ms Bauman?

WOMAN : No, any time during office hours.

OPERATOR : Right. I'll see they get the message.

WOMAN : Thank you. Goodbye.

OPERATOR : Goodbye.

....

OPERATOR : Manchester Exhibition Centre.

MAN : Good morning. My name is Mr Archibald of Quick Copy. Could I speak to Mrs Hutchinson in Printing Services?

OPERATOR : Hold on please. I'll put you through.

....

Sorry, there's no reply. Can I take a message?

MAN : Yes please. Could you tell her that the TC107 photocopier we were to deliver is not available, at least for the time being, but we've got the TC108A. Would she like us to deliver that instead? It's a little more expensive, but it's a better machine.

OPERATOR : Right. Your name again is....

MAN : Archibald. She has my number. She can get me on extension 13.

OPERATOR : Right.

MAN : Thank you. Goodbye.

OPERATOR : Goodbye.

....

OPERATOR : Manchester Exhibition Centre.

WOMAN : Hello. My name's Julie Shaw. I saw your ad in the Manchester Echo for the post of receptionist. It says to get in touch with Mr Hawkins for further details.

OPERATOR : Yes. Hold the line, please.

....

Sorry. There's no reply.

WOMAN : Oh, well, could you ask him to send a job description and application form, please?

OPERATOR : Yes. Your name is...

WOMAN : Julie Shaw, 47 Heathfield Gardens, Trafford, Manchester ME4 SY2.

OPERATOR : 47, Heathfield Gardens, Trafford, Manchester...and the post code again, please?

WOMAN : ME4 SY2.

OPERATOR : Right. You should get them within the next couple of days.

WOMAN : Thank you very much. Goodbye.

OPERATOR : Goodbye.

....

OPERATOR : Manchester Exhibition Centre.

WOMAN : Good morning. I'd like to speak to Mr Taylor in the Stand Hire Section, please.

OPERATOR : I'm sorry there's no one in at the moment. Can I help?

WOMAN : Yes, well, perhaps. My name's Mrs Rogers from Cambridge Infotec. We've hired some space for the next Information Technology Exhibition and I wanted to know how many power points would be available.

OPERATOR : Right. I'll ask.

WOMAN : And how many telephone lines we'll have at our disposal.

OPERATOR : Telephone lines.....Right. I've made a note of that. What did you say your name was?

WOMAN : Rogers. Mrs Susan Rogers of Cambridge Infotec. It's Mr Taylor, I think, who I 've spoken to before.

OPERATOR : Right. I'll pass on your questions to him.

WOMAN : Thank you. Goodbye.

OPERATOR : Goodbye.

UNIT 6

MRS WILLIS : Hello, dear. Have a nice day?

MR WILLIS : Much the same as usual. What about you?

MRS WILLIS : Busy as always. I've just got in myself. I haven't had a chance to check the answerphone yet.

MR WILLIS : O.K. I'll do it. Now, where have I put my pen....Ah! Here it is. Right.

JIM : Wednesday. 8.30. Jim speaking. Just off for the airport. Wanted to confirm that it's O.K. for lunch tomorrow. Twelve thirty at the Brewer's Arms as arranged. Sorry to bother you at home but I know you're at the Motor Show all week and I don't have the number of your stand. I'm booked in at the Royal George Hotel, Newbury Street. Phone or leave a message if there's a problem at your end. I haven't got the hotel number on me but you'll find it in the directory. Bye.

MAN : Hello..er...Murdoch's Garage here. We've looked for the oil leak and I'm afraid it's worse than you thought. It means leaving the car with us for at least three days. So, do you want to pick it up at 6pm tomorrow as arranged and make another appointment, or shall we keep it and do the repairs now? We won't do anything till we hear from you. Goodbye.

MRS GROVES : Pamela Groves of International Travel here. Just to tell you we've got you a booking for the 15th. Your tickets are ready and you can collect them when you like. We couldn't get you on the 6.30 flight, but since you gave us an hour or so either way, we've got you two seats on the 7.45 plane. Flight number 647. Check in at the airport by 7.15 at the latest. Thank you. Goodbye.

JIM : Jim here again. Problem, I'm afraid. The planes have been grounded because of fog. They might be grounded for some time, so, if it's all right with you, can we meet at the same place, same time, but the day after tomorrow? Phone the Royal George if you can't make it. Thanks. Bye.

MAGGIE : Hello darlings. This is Aunt Maggie. Er....Oh dear, I hate these answering machines. I never know what to say. Still, one must move with the times, I suppose. Anyway, I'm ringing to say that I shall be in London for the day tomorrow and I'd love it if both of you could come and have lunch with me at The King's Head. James and his wife — you remember James, don't you? — Well, they wanted me to stay overnight but I can't leave Ken alone for too long because of his arthritis, so...well, anyway, I'll be in all this evening so please ring and say if you're free for lunch tomorrow. I do hope you are. We'll arrange the time when I hear from you. Sorry, I must ring off now — Ken is calling. Bye. Coming, Ken !

MR WILLIS : My God! Doesn't she realise I've only got one side of a cassette for the day's messages ? What's next?

RITA : Hello, June. Rita here. Sorry to let you down, but I just can't make it for babysitting on Friday. I've got a...well, never mind, I'll tell you later. But I just wanted to warn you now so ...anyway, I'm really sorry but, well, I'll tell you later. Bye.

MR WILLIS : Damn ! That means we'll have to cancel the theatre. Let's see if there's anything else on the tape...

JIM : Jim again. Look, I've decided to get an overnight train instead, so I'll be there by tomorrow morning. But I think I'd still prefer to meet the day after tomorrow if it's all right with you — a night on the train isn't the best thing just before a meeting. However, if you can't change the date, we can still make it tomorrow if necessary. Let me know as soon as possible. O.K. Thanks. Bye.

JAMES : Hello. Mr Willis? James Stewart here. I don't know if you remember but I called at the stand yesterday. I was interested in the four-wheel drive model for our Safari Park in Kenya. I'm sorry to bother you at home but you said I could if necessary. I did call your stand at the Motor Show but they couldn't find you. Anyway, I am definitely interested. It would mean a first order of 12 vehicles and perhaps more to follow. Could you ring me at the Hotel International some time this evening? I'm leaving for Kenya tomorrow afternoon. Thank you. Goodbye.

MR WILLIS : Great ! Well, that seems to be it. Now all I've got to do is sort out my timetable.... Hmm. 12 four-wheel drive models.

UNIT 8

Conversation 1

WOMAN : Gas Board. Can I help you?

WESTON : Yes, please. It's about the bill I've just received...

WOMAN : One moment, please. I'll put you through.

MAN : Customer accounts. Can I help you?

WESTON : Yes, I hope so. It's about the bill I've just received.

MAN : Can I have your customer number please?

WESTON : Er....Oh yes, I see...it's 397-stroke-4988B.

MAN : Just one moment ,please. Right. Mr Weston. Is that right?

WESTON : Yes. Now, I think there's been a slight mistake.

MAN : £495.75p.

WESTON : Yes. Well, that's what the bill says. But you must have slipped up somewhere.

MAN : Your meter was read on the 25th of last month. Is that correct?

WESTON : I really can't remember. Look, the point is, there seems to be an error in your accounts somewhere.

MAN : Well, the figures look all right to me, Mr Weston. If you multiply the number of units by the unit cost...

WESTON : Yes, yes. But what I'm questioning is the actual number of units I'm supposed to have used.

MAN : I see. Well, the best thing is if we send someone round to check the meter again. Just one moment. I'll put you through to the right department.

WESTON : Thank you.

Conversation 3

GORDON : So, you think the meeting went well last week?

WOMAN : Yes, but there are one or two points....

GORDON : Oh. I'm sorry. I'd better go and find a phone. So sorry.

WOMAN : That's all right. I'll have a look at the menu.

......

GORDON : Right. I'm really sorry about that. Have you ordered?

WOMAN : Yes, about ten minutes ago. I think you'd better order quickly or else...

GORDON : Yes. Quite. Oh no ! Not again ! Please forgive me. I'll be right back.

WOMAN : Shall I order something for you? Oh dear.

Conversation 4

GORDON : Damn, damn, damn ! I'll never make it by 4 o'clock with all this traffic. I'd better ring Morrison's.

DOWNING : Hello. Morrison's.

GORDON : Hello. Is that Mr Downing?

DOWNING : Yes. Speaking.

GORDON : This is Gordon Phillips here, Mr Downing.

DOWNING : Oh yes. Good afternoon, Mr Phillips.

GORDON : Look, I really must apologise. I' m speaking from my car and I'm stuck in a terrible traffic jam on the ring road. Would you mind very much if we made our appointment at 5 instead of 4. I'm sure I'll be there by then. I'm terribly sorry.

DOWNING : Don't mention it. It's quite all right. Come when you can. I'll be waiting for you.

GORDON : Thank you very much. I'll see you as soon as I can then. Goodbye.

DOWNING : Goodbye.

GORDON : Good. I'd better warn Joan too.....

JOAN : 64933.

GORDON : Hello, darling, it's me. Listen, don't expect me before 7 this evening. I'm in a traffic jam and I've had to postpone one appointment already, so I really don't think...

JOAN : Don't worry, darling. It doesn't matter. I'll expect you when I see you.

GORDON : Right. Sorry, darling. Bye.

JOAN : Bye.

GORDON : One more call....

PETER : Johnson and Phillips.

GORDON : Peter? This is Gordon. Look, I'm sorry to bother you, but I'm expecting a phone call from those people in the States about 5.30 and I don't think I'm going to be there in time to take it. Could you deal with it, do you think?

PETER : Yes, of course, Gordon. No problem.

GORDON : Thanks a lot, Peter. The file's on my desk. I'll be there as soon as I can.

PETER : O.K. Don't worry about it. Bye.

GORDON : Bye.

UNIT 9

Conversation 2

RECEPTION : Reception.

MAN : This is Mr Hargreaves, Room 314. I'd like some information about the London-by-night tour that starts from the hotel every evening.

RECEPTION : Yes, Mr Hargreaves. Well, there should be a brochure about it on the desk in your room.

MAN : Yes, there is. But it doesn't say anything about where you go or what you can see. Could you tell me exactly what the tour consists of?

RECEPTION : Well, I'm afraid not, Mr Hargreaves. It's supposed to be a sort of mystery tour. I think the brochure does say that. But I can tell you that many of our guests have taken the tour and none of them has ever complained.

MAN : Oh, I see. Well, thank you very much.

RECEPTION : Pleasure, sir. Goodb...

MAN : Oh, and there's one more thing. How often do you change the cabaret show here? You see, I was here two months ago and I saw the show then, so I don't really want to see the same one again.

RECEPTION : Well, large parts of it are changed every month, Mr Hargreaves. You might see one or two numbers that are the same, but most of the show will be completely different.

MAN : Oh good. And how long does it go on for ?

RECEPTION : I'm not sure, sir. I believe it tells you in the brochure, doesn't it?

MAN : Oh. Right. I'll have a look. Thank you.

RECEPTION : Thank you, sir.

Conversation 3

RECEPTION : Lincoln Hotel. Good afternoon.

WOMAN : Good afternoon. I'd like to enquire about renting conference rooms.

RECEPTION : Yes, madam. Well, we have three rooms, all about the same size.....do you have our brochure on conference facilities?

WOMAN : No, I don't. Is it illustrated ? I mean, does it give one a good idea of the size and look of the rooms?

RECEPTION : Oh yes, madam. You'll find everything you need. Including a full list of prices.

WOMAN : Fine. Well, could you send me one please? I'm Marion Westbury...

RECEPTION : Yes.

WOMAN : Industrial Marketing...

RECEPTION : Yes.

WOMAN : 59, Queen's Terrace, Redhill, Surrey.

RECEPTION : Right, Ms Westbury. I'll get one in the post to you today.

WOMAN : Thank you very much. Goodbye.

RECEPTION : Goodbye.

Guidelines

1

The F.T. Index at close : up five point three to thirteen point nine. British Electric lost two points, upset by a privatisation setback.

2

At the third stroke, the time sponsored by Accurist will be nine thirty-two precisely. At the third stroke, the time sponsored by Accurist will be nine thirty-two and ten seconds.

3

Lovers of classical music will be delighted by the Viennese evening at the Barbican Hall in the Barbican Centre. The London Symphony Orchestra will play many of the Strauss family waltzes and polkas. The concert begins at nineteen forty-five hours.

4

This is from British Telecom's album of the week : Backyard Blues by New Horizon. The title of the track : Name of the Game which, as a single, is already number 13 in the charts this week.

5

...And then, the little brown rabbit knocked at the door. "Come in" said a voice which sounded very strange....

6

A lane closure on the southbound carriageway of the M25 is causing severe delays. Drivers are advised to choose an alternative route between junctions 5 and 7.

7

And finally, the three-thirty. First, number seven, King Harry, five to two; eight, Hobson's Choice, evens favourite; five, Orange Delight, eight to one. Non-runner, number twelve. Eleven ran.

8

...And England and France have qualified for the final to be played in Spain next month. Here at home, this evening's match between Manchester United and Liverpool has been cancelled because of snow.

9

In a statement in the House of Commons yesterday, the Prime Minister said that it was not necessarily in this country's interest to maintain a peace-keeping force in the disputed territory.

10

During the day, the rain will clear from the west. It will be generally mild this morning but will turn colder as the rain clears.

11

This is Brian Craven with you for the next hour on Capital, bringing you some "Oldies but Goldies". And our next request, from Maureen and John in Croydon, is for Andy Williams singing "Almost There".

12

Jakes did some wonderful batting until he was finally caught by Wilson for 125. His biggest score this season. When they stopped for tea, the West Indies were 209 for 3.

UNIT 10

1

WOMAN : But you should have received the goods last week, Mr Bryant.

MAN : Well, I didn't. Are you sure you haven't made a mistake with the address?

WOMAN : Just one moment. I'll check....Here we are. James Bryant, 155, Wilton Drive, Man...

MAN : No, it's 55, not 155.

WOMAN : Oh, I'm terribly sorry, Mr Bryant, ...

2

MAN : Fire Brigade? Quick ! There's a fire at Rose Cottage.

WOMAN : Rose Cottage.

MAN : Yes. You know, it's just on the edge of the wood.

WOMAN : Which wood, sir?

MAN : Please hurry ! There are people inside !

WOMAN : Please calm down sir ! Now,...

3

WOMAN : And what have you got in Greece?

MAN : Well, there are eight tours altogether. If you'd like to come in and see us, I can give you all the details and show you the brochures.

WOMAN : I'm afraid I can't this week. Could you...

4

MAN : Palmer. That's 'P'...

WOMAN : 'B' for Benjamin?

MAN : No, 'P'.

WOMAN : Sorry?

MAN : 'P' for...er....pyjamas.

WOMAN : Chalmers, did you say? I'm afraid there's no Mr Chalmers working here.

MAN : No, ...

5

MAN : 478993

WOMAN : Hello, could I...oh...did you say "478993"?

MAN : That's right, yes.

WOMAN : Oh, I'm terribly sorry,...

6

WOMAN : Is it ringing?

MAN : Wait a minute...No, it's engaged.

WOMAN : Oh no ! Well, look, we'll go a bit further and try again later from another call box.

MAN : O.K. Now, how do I get my money back?

WOMAN : Well, you just...

7

WOMAN : 577431

MAN : Er...hello...I've just moved into the area and I haven't had to see a...a...doctor here before...

WOMAN : And you want to be put on Doctor Thorpe's list or Doctor Richards' list?

MAN : Well, the point is, I've got this terrible pain in my stomach. It's...it's really bad and...

8

MAN : Sales department.

WOMAN : Oh no ! I asked for the accounts department.

MAN : Just one moment. I'll have you transferred.

GIRL : Marketing.

WOMAN : Aren't you the accounts department ?

GIRL : No. I think you've got the wrong extension. Just one moment.

MAN : Sales department.

WOMAN : What? Listen, I think...

CORRIGÉ

UNIT 1

Conversation

1. ring them up 2. make a call 3. get through
4. telephoned 5. code number 6. figures
7. dialling code booklet 8. receiver
9. dialling tone 10. buttons 11. dial
12. busy 13. engaged 14. hang up
15. call back 16. get through 17. exchange
18. operator 19. transferred charge
20. transferred charge 21. hold the line
22. put you through

A. 212 578 9644 B. 212 C. 01 D. 061
E. 010 1 F. 155 G. 212 578 9644
H. 375338 I. 375338 J. 578 9644

Practice

cord :2 handset :3 button :5
digital display :6 cradle :1 socket :8
loudspeaker :4 lamp :7
extension lines :9

Practice

(words in order of appearance in text)

area code directory look up
Yellow Pages Directory Enquiries
receiver* tone dial
handset* Hold on switchboard
extension number

** Note that "receiver" and "handset" are interchangeable here.*

UNIT 2

Conversation 1 : comprehension

1. The Frenchman mispronounces the name "Tyler" as if it were "Teelair". He then spells his own name using the French pronunciation of the letters. "A" in French sounds rather like "R" in English. "I" in French is like "E" in English. "M" is the same, but "é" sounds like "A" in English.

2. The probable outcome is that Mr Tyler will have no idea who has called since "Rema" doesn't look or sound anything like "Aimé". Therefore, Mr Aimé won't receive a phone call as he expects.

Conversation 2

1. Sorry, wrong number 2. That's quite all right
3. Could you speak up a little 4. I was wondering
5. Could you be more specific
6. gain access to databases
7. linked to a network 8. isn't it
9. Actually 10. electronic mail
11. I don't know what/means
12. is it 13. That's right 14. Shall I
15. by all means 16. isn't it 17. in fact
18. give us a ring

A. Simon Wright, 130 Pigeon Lane, Felixstowe, Suffolk FX3 2HY. B. FX3 2HY.

UNIT 3

Conversation

1. change 2. coins 3. slot
4. Take the phone off the hook 5. purring
6. hum 7. it sounds all right
8. the minimum fee 9. Is it ringing
10. it doesn't sound like it 11. speaking
12. call box 13. the pips
14. We've been cut off

A. Lift handset B. Margate
C. a couple of minutes D. second exit on the left E. Alma Road
F. down Stanley road G. a crossroads H. straight ahead
I. half a mile J. filling station K. church
L. youth M. roundabout N. town hall
D. William Street P. health clinic O. right-hand side

Practice

1. put in: insert pick up: lift
carry on: continue put through: connect
put back: replace

2. Replace the handset (receiver). Collect your refund: (if you have put in three, 10p coins, you will not get a refund; if you have included three 2p coins, you will get 6p back; if you have included two 5p coins, you will get 5p back). Lift the handset, listen for the dial tone, insert your money and dial.

3. It depends on what coins you put in. If you have put in two 20p coins, you will get nothing back. If you have included a 10p coin and one or more 5p coins, you will get 10p back. If you have included a 10p coin and one or more 2p coins, you will get the full refund of 12p.

UNIT 4

Conversation 1: comprehension

Ian McIntosh,
19, Ruthrieston Road,
Kingswells
(Scotland)
Tel: 0244 34899

Conversation 2

1. extension 2. hold on 3. switchboard
4. I'm afraid 5. get back 6. agenda
7. divert 8. is to take place 9. fire away
10. crossed 11. interference
12. videoconference 13. Freefone number
14. Will do 15. Thanks for calling

Practice

1. False: if you want a Freefone number, the Freefone subscriber pays, not the caller. There is no charge to the caller for accepted transferred charge calls either.

2. False: you can book them at any time, but it is **preferable** to call before 10.30pm for an early morning call.

3. True: There is a fee for each call as well as the cost of the card.

4. True: "The service is good for business". A private individual would have little to gain from being a Freephone subscriber.

5. False: you use it when you want to know how much **you** will have to pay.

6. False: Before the charge is transferred, the person you are calling has to accept the call.

UNIT 5

Conversation 1 : comprehension

(Possible completed message pad)

Date:	4th March
Time:	12.45
Message for:	Mr Gordon
Caller's name:	Jeffrey *(or Geoffrey)* Paxton
Tel:	Ext 54. Digital Electronics.

MESSAGE
Re: estimate for new switchboard sent over a month ago. Mr Paxton requires decision quickly because of need to plan work schedule. Could you call him back as soon as possible?

Conversation 2: comprehension

(possible messages)

1.

Date:	4th March
Time:	12.50
Message for:	Stand Hire Section
Caller's name:	Jane Bauman
Tel.	3875929

MESSAGE
Enquiry about hiring 50 sq. metres floor space, Textile Machinery Exhibition, April. Please ring back with information during office hours.

2.

Date:	4th March
Time:	12.55
Message for:	Mrs Hutchinson, Printing Services
Caller's name:	Mr Archibald
Tel:	Quick Copy. Ext 13

MESSAGE
TC107 Photocopier not available. Mr Archibald suggests TC108A instead — more expensive but better machine. Please call him back.

3.

Date:	4th March
Time:	13.00
Message for:	Mr Hawkins
Caller's name:	Julie Shaw
Tel:	

MESSAGE
Applicant for receptionist post. Please send job description and application form:
47, Heathfield Gardens
Trafford
Manchester ME 4 SV2

4.

Date:	4th March
Time:	13.05
Message for:	Mr Taylor, Stand Hire Section.
Caller's name:	Mrs Susan Rogers, Cambrige Infotec.
Tel:	

MESSAGE
Re: space hired for information Technology Exhibition. Please inform Mrs Rogers of number of power points and phone lines available.

Practice

hold facility: possibilité de mettre en attente un correspondant
loudspeaker: haut-parleur
extension: poste
lamp signalling: témoins lumineux
conference facility: faculté de faire participer un collaborateur à la conversation
exchange lines: lignes réseau
transfer facility: possibilité de transférer une communication
button: touche

2 • interrupt facility • dialling with the receiver in the cradle

3 • visual display showing numbers dialled, the date and time • electronic memory • call-timer

UNIT 6

Conversation: comprehension

1. Jim had arranged a meeting with Mr Willis for tomorrow. He's coming from a long way away (probably Scotland because of the "overnight train") and had planned to fly. Because of flight delays he first of all puts off the meeting until the day after tomorrow. Then, he decides to take the overnight train instead of the plane. This means he will arrive tomorrow but, because travelling overnight by train is not always restful, Jim thinks the day after tomorrow would be better for the meeting. He asks Mr Willis to confirm.

2. Mr Willis works for a motor-car manufacturer or distributor. He could be a salesman or even a sales manager.

3. He's going to call Aunt Maggie and James Stewart. (Note: He's not going to call Jim until tomorrow. It's probably too late to call Murdoch's garage. He doesn't need to call the travel agency — he simply has to pick up the tickets. The babysitter doesn't need calling back either).

4. They're almost certainly going to stay at home. They had planned to go to the theatre but the babysitter, Rita, has got other plans.

5. • Murdoch's want to keep the car for at least three days.
• Lunch with Jim to be confirmed: same time and place but the day after tomorrow instead of tomorrow.
• Mr Stewart definitely wants to order 12 vehicles.

Practice

1. ... want to record your announcement.
2. ... want to listen to your messages.
3. ... want to accept a call while the machine is on.
4. ... want the machine to record messages while you are out.
5. ... have finished recording your announcement.
6. ... the message cassette has come to the end.
7. ... the answer function is operating.
8. ... there are messages for you to listen to.
9. ... someone is calling.
10. ... listen to your messages by means of a remote control device.
11. ... there are no beeps on the announcement tape.
12. ... a flashing sign tells you to "change cassette".

UNIT 7

Conversation

1. May I ask who's calling, please
2. you must have seen
3. ask you a few questions 4. expect
5. Would you mind telling me
6. don't you think 7. Don't you find
8. we're thinking of putting in
9. it sounds interesting 10. Do you mind if I ask you
11. Why don't we ask him to drop in 12. Wouldn't it
13. doesn't commit you to anything
14. Shall we make it tomorrow evening
15. as you like 16. it's up to you
17. What about a quarter to eight

Practice

(possible completed text)

1. Prestel enables you to gain **instant access** to both **information** and **services**. What it does basically is to **link** your telephone line to your **microcomputer** or your **television**, which means that you can **call up** this information at any time of the day or night and see **it displayed on the screen**. If you decide to **subscribe** to Prestel, you will have to pay for **access** to the network but most of the **information pages** are free.

2. Not mentioned in the text are: weather forecasts, where-to-eat guides, consumer advice.
Services mentioned that are not on the list: house-hunting, teleshopping, financial information services, telex.

3. Prestel subscription: quarterly standing charge
Connection to Prestel network: time charge.
Information pages: either free or price per page displayed.
Telephone call charges: charged at local rate.
Telex: sender pays between £1 and £4 per hundred words (depending on the destination).

UNIT 8

Conversation 1: comprehension

1. 397/4988B
2. £495.75
3. Because the peson who read the meter probably made a mistake.
4. • I think there's been a slight mistake • you must have slipped up somewhere • there seems to be an error • what I'm questioning is...
5. He's polite and in control. He avoids saying "You're wrong" and prefers to use more polite, impersonal suggestions of error on the part of the Gas Board.

Conversation 2

1. What's up 2. I'm getting fed up
3. It's about time 4. I've had enough
5. Why on earth not 6. I wish you'd hurry up
7. This is the last straw

Conversations 3 & 4: comprehension

1. • I'm sorry • So sorry • I'm really sorry about that • Please forgive me* • I really must apologise* • I'm terribly sorry • Sorry • I'm sorry to bother you

* Formal expressions. The others can be used both formally and informally.

2. • That's all right • Don't mention it • It's quite all right • Don't worry • It doesn't matter • No problem • Don't worry about it.

Practice

1. A sun roof is a panel that can be opened in the roof of a car.
To call base means to call home or call your office when you're out.
If you've run out of money, it means that you had some money to start with but now you haven't got any left.
Two-digit dialling means that when you make calls to those numbers that are stored in memory, there is a two-figure code for each number. This saves time in dialling.
Pre-programmed numbers are those telephone numbers that you have stored in the memory bank of the telephone's computer.
A "hands-free" facility means that you don't have to hold the receiver when you're phoning someone. Your hands are free.
To "put to good use" means to use in the best or the most profitable way.
2. The advantages of a carphone may be summarised as follows:
- You don't have to:
  - waste time looking for a phone box if you need to make a call.
  - make calls to your office from a client's phone.
  - waste time when you arrive at the client's office. (You can phone to tell him exactly when you will be arriving, so he can be there to meet you.
- You can:
  - make appropriate phone calls immediately if you hear some important business news on your car radio.
  - warn the people concerned immediately if you get stuck in a traffic jam, and delayed.
  - hold meetings by phone in the car.

Practice

(from the top left-hand corner reading left to right and ending in the bottom right-hand corner)

• A sailor is calling a sailor on another ship. Normally one can ask for a "person-to-person" call in the United States.

• A man about to commit suicide is calling the Samaritans, an organisation that helps people in trouble.

• A balloonist has received a call from a double-glazing salesperson.

• A bricklayer is calling one of his workmates.

• A train driver is calling the station where he'll be stopping next. (The quality of food and drink on British Rail trains is a standard joke in England).

• The foreman on a building site is ordering tea from a café.

• A man, faced with armed robbery in the street, is calling 999 — emergency services.

• A man in hospital is phoning the grocer's to order some grapes.

• "Beam me up Scotty" — an allusion to the television series "Startrek". The Captain of the Starship Enterprise wants to be "teleported" from planet Earth to the Starship.

• A woman driver is phoning a friend in Tokyo and comparing traffic conditions.

• The driver of a sports car is probably calling his wife or girlfriend — just for the sake of using the carphone.

• A woman passenger in a jet flying over the Indian Ocean is phoning either to the people who are expecting her, or to her family at home. Disaster has struck but she doesn't seem too concerned.

• A vicar has got a direct line to God !

• A taxi driver is complaining to someone about cell phones. He calls them "cellular phones" by mistake.

• A policeman is calling the chiropodist. (The policeman's been on his feet all day.)

• A doctor is giving a patient advice while walking along the street.

• A man who has not got a "hands-free" facility has been called by his wife (or other member of his family).

• A businessman with two cellphones is behaving as if he were in his office.

• A traffic warden has received a call (probably by the man who wants to commit suicide) meant for the Samaritans. (Traffic wardens do not have a reputation for being very helpful !)

• A woman is phoning the telephone company. Ironically, she is using a fairly expensive piece of equipment, yet she is complaining about her phone bill.

UNIT 9

Conversation 1

1. Can I help you
2. Could you tell me what you charge
3. Can you give me both prices
4. Is breakfast included
5. How long in advance 6. Say
7. Three weeks beforehand 8. Not at all

Conversation 2: comprehension

1. It says that the London-by-night tour is a mystery tour and starts from the hotel every evening.

2. It gives the length of the cabaret show (and almost certainly what time it starts). It probably says that large parts of the show are changed every month (since the reception clerk knows this).

Conversation 3: comprehension

1. The hotel brochure on conference facilities. It is fully illustrated, and a price list is included.

2. Marion Westbury, Industrial Marketing, 59 Queen's Terrace, Redhill, Surrey.

3. • I'd like to enquire about... • does it give one a good idea of • I'll get one in the post to you today.

Conversation 4

1. booking 2. Single room with shower
3. that's the point 4. at the full rate
5. reduced rate 6. How much more would it be
7. Would you like me to give you 8. I'm afraid not
9. That's quite all right.

Practice

1/A: The information is about the F.T. index.

2/C: The voice is giving the correct time.

3/F: The information is about an event at the Barbican Centre in London.

4/H: The recorded information is about the hit parade/the charts.

5/G: The voice is telling a bedtime story for children.

6/I : The message concerns traffic problems in the south of England.

7/D: The message is giving racing results: the names of the first three horses and their "odds".

8/E: An announcement about football matches, both international and at home.

9/J : An extract of the political news.

10/L : A taped weather forecast.

11/K : An extract from a radio programme - the disc jockey is playing requests.

12/G : Cricket scores. (You can tell it's cricket because of "batting", "caught by", "stopped for tea" and "209 for 3" — all words and phrases from cricket.)

UNIT 10

Conversations: comprehension

1.

1. Mr Bryant hasn't received some goods he ordered. He thinks they've sent the goods to the wrong address.
2. A man has seen a fire in a cottage and is phoning the Fire Brigade. He's particularly concerned because he thinks there are people trapped inside.
3. A woman wants information about holidays in Greece. She's phoning a travel agent.
4. A man is trying to ring a certain Mr Palmer at his office. The switchboard is having problems understanding the name.
5. A wrong number.
6. A couple are on their way somewhere and are trying to ring someone from a call box, possibly the person they're going to see.
7. A man has got a terrible pain in his stomach. He hasn't got his own doctor in the area, so he's ringing a local doctor for an urgent appointment.
8. A woman is trying to get through to the accounts department of a company. She keeps getting transferred to the wrong extension.

2.

(possible completed sentences).

1. ... I'm sure the goods will be sent back to us — in that case, I'll get them off to your correct address as soon as I can.
2. ... can I have your name and the exact location of the fire please?
3. ... send the brochures to me with a complete price list?
4. ... it's "P" for Peter: Palmer. (Would you like me to spell it for you?).
5. ... I must have dialled the wrong number.
6. ... put down the receiver and it refunds the money automatically.
7. ... I'd like an appointment as soon as possible, please.
8. ... I spoke to you a few seconds ago. (I wanted the accounts department but you transferred me to the marketing department who transferred me back to you !)

Vocabulary

1. directory 2. slot 3. pips
4. putting/through 5. hold on 6. interference
7. alarm call 8. cradle 9. beep
10. rewind 11. standing charge 12. digit

Matching

1/D 2/F 3/C 4/E 5/H 6/J 7/G
8/A 9/I 10/B

Invention

(possible conversation)

SWITCHBOARD : General Electronics. Good afternoon*.

DAVID : Good afternoon. Could I speak to Elizabeth North, please ?

SWITCHBOARD : Hold the line please.

...

I'm afraid her line is engaged at the moment.

DAVID : Could I hold please ?**

SWITCHBOARD : Certainly, sir.

...

The line's free now, sir. I'm putting you through.

DAVID : Thank you.

SECRETARY : Elizabeth North's office.

DAVID : Is that you, Elizabeth?

SECRETARY : No, I'm afraid she's just left the office.

DAVID : Oh. Well, could you give me her home number, do you think ?

SECRETARY : I'm terribly sorry, sir, but I'm not really allowed to do that. Who's speaking please ?

DAVID : This is David Marks. I'm phoning from New York and it's really rather important that I get in touch with Elizabeth as soon as possible.

SECRETARY : I see. Well, perhaps I can take a message?

DAVID : Thank you. Yes. Could you tell her that I've been delayed in New York until Sunday, so I won't be able to meet her as planned in Paris on Friday. I've got some urgent family problems to settle. Could you ask her if she can be in Paris on Monday ? And could she ring me as soon as possible to confirm or fix another date ?

SECRETARY : Right, Mr Marks. I'll see that she gets it first thing tomorrow morning.

DAVID : Thank you so much. Goodbye.

SECRETARY : Goodbye.

MESSAGE

David Marks called from New York. Delayed in New York by family problems until Sunday. Can't make meeting in Paris on Friday. Suggests Monday. Please call him to confirm or fix another date.

* Given the time difference between New York and London, it is almost certain to be the afternoon in London when David phones.

** American usage.

LEXIQUE

A

to accept a call accepter (de payer) une communication en PCV

advice of duration and/or charge (ADC) possibilité de savoir la durée et le prix d'une communication en passant par la standardiste

alarm call réveil par téléphone

ambulance service ambulances

to announce annoncer

announcement annonce

to answer répondre

answerphone répondeur

area code indicatif

B

beep bip sonore

bill facture
- telephone bill facture de téléphone

bleep signal sonore, "bip"

booklet livret
- dialling code booklet livret des indicatifs

to book réserver

box boîte, cabine
- call box/phone box cabine téléphonique

built-in microphone micro incorporé

busy occupé

button touche

C

cable câble

call appel
- alarm call réveil par téléphone
- early morning call réveil par téléphone
- emergency call appel d'urgence
- failed call appel qui n'aboutit pas
- follow-on call appel renouvelé
- local call communication urbaine
- long-distance call appel interurbain
- operator call communication établie par l'opératrice
- outgoing call communication vers l'extérieur
- reverse charge call appel en PCV

to call appeler
- to call back rappeler
- to call base appeler le siège
- to call collect (Amer.) appeler en PCV
- to call up (information) accéder (aux renseignements)

call box cabine téléphonique

call timer minuteur

card carte
- credit card carte de crédit

cassette cassette
- message cassette cassette pour enregistrer les messages

Cellphone radiotéléphone (téléphone sans fil)

charge tarif
- free of charge gratuit
- quarterly standing charge abonnement trimestriel
- time charge tarification selon le temps d'utilisation

to charge faire payer

code code
- area code indicatif
- dialling code booklet livret des indicatifs
- post code code postal

coin pièce de monnaie

coinbox cabine téléphonique

to communicate communiquer

communications satellite satellite de transmission

conference facility possibilité d'avoir une conférence à trois ou à plusieurs

to connect brancher, relier, joindre

control contrôle
- remote control télécommande

cord cordon

cordless sans cordon

correspondent interlocuteur, correspondant

cradle berceau

credit card carte de crédit

crossed line ligne embrouillée

to cut off couper
- to be cut off être coupé

D

device dispositif, appareil

dial cadran
- dial tone tonalité

to dial composer un numéro
  two-digit dialling numérotation abrégée (2 chiffres)
  dialling code booklet livret des indicatifs
digit chiffre
  digital display affichage à cristaux liquides
  two-digit dialling (voir "to dial")
directory annuaire
  Directory Enquiries Renseignements
display
  digital display (voir "digit")
  visual display affichage
to divert renvoyer (des appels sur un autre poste)
duration durée
  advice of duration... (voir "advice")

E

early morning call réveil par téléphone
electronic électronique
  electronic mail messagerie électronique
  electronic mail facility possibilité de messagerie électronique
  electronic mailbox boîte à lettres électronique
  electronic memory mémoire électronique
emergency urgence
  emergency call appel d'urgence
  emergency service urgences
engaged occupé
to enquire se renseigner
  Directory Enquiries Renseignements
entertainment service service loisirs
exchange central
  exchange line ligne réseau
extension poste
  extension line poste
  priority extension poste prioritaire

F

facility possibilité
failed call appel qui n'aboutit pas
fee tarif, taxe
  minimum fee tarif/taxe minimum
figure chiffre
Fire Brigade Pompiers
flashing qui clignote
follow-on call appel renouvelé
  follow-on call button touche pour relancer une communication
frame cadre
  response frame cadre de réponse
Freefone numéro vert
free gratuit
  free of charge gratuit

G

General Post Office PTT
to gain access to accéder
to get joindre
to get in touch with contacter
to get through obtenir une communication
to give someone a ring appeler quelqu'un
Guidelines bulletins et services (voir Unit 9)

H

handset combiné
hands-free facility possibilité de parler et d'écouter sans avoir le combiné en main
to hang up raccrocher
hardware matériel
high-pitched aigu
hold attente
  to put a call on hold mettre un appel en attente
  hold facility possibilité de mise en attente
to hold on ne pas quitter, rester en ligne
to hold the line rester en ligne
home banking gestion électronique de son compte en banque
home number numéro personnel
off the hook décroché
hum bourdonnement

I

incoming message message de l'extérieur
information renseignements
  information service service d'informations
  information provider serveur
to insert insérer
to instal installer
interference parasites
interrupt facility possibilité d'intervention sur un poste en communication

K

key touche
keyboard clavier

L

lamp témoin lumineux
  lamp signalling témoins lumineux signalant l'état d'occupation de chaque ligne
to lay a cable poser un câble
to lift décrocher (le combiné)
line ligne
  crossed lines lignes embrouillées
  exchange line ligne réseau
  extension line poste
  telephone/phone line ligne téléphonique
  telex line ligne telex
to be listed figurer dans l'annuaire
local call appel urbain
long-distance call appel interurbain

to look up chercher (un numéro dans l'annuaire)
loudspeaker hautparleur

M

mail courrier
  electronic mail messagerie électronique
mailbox boîte aux lettres
  electronic mailbox boîte aux lettres électronique
to make a call appeler, téléphoner
message message
  incoming message message d'un appelant
  message cassette cassette pour enregistrer les messages
microcomputer ordinateur, micro-ordinateur
microphone microphone
  built-in microphone microphone incorporé
minimum fee tarif/taxe minimum
model modèle
modem modem

N

network réseau
number numéro
  pre-programmed number numéro pré-programmé, numéro en mémoire
  wrong number faux numéro, erreur

O

operator standardiste, opératrice
  operator call appel qui passe par l'opératrice
  operator services services "grand public"
outgoing call appel vers l'extérieur

P

password mot de passe
payphone cabine téléphonique
paytone tonalité
phone téléphone, appareil
phone line ligne
phone card télécarte
to phone téléphoner
to pick up (the phone, etc.) décrocher
the pips bip sonore
to play back écouter (une cassette de messages)
post code code postal
Post Office bureau de poste, PTT
pre-programmed number numéro pré-programmé, numéro en mémoire
to press appuyer
press-button telephone appareil à touches
Prestel Minitel (équivalent approximatif)
priority extension poste prioritaire
purring ronronnement
to put a call on hold mettre un appel en attente
to put in insérer
to put someone through mettre en communication

Q

quarterly standing charge abonnement trimestriel

R

range portée
rate taux
receiver combiné
receptionist réceptionniste
to record enregistrer
refund remboursement
to refund rembourser
remote control télécommande
to replace remettre en place
reply réponse
to require avoir besoin de
response frame cadre de réponse
reverse charge call appel en PCV
to ring appeler, sonner
  to ring off raccrocher
  to ring up appeler
  ringing tone tonalité (quand le numéro sonne)

S

saturated saturé
screen écran
signal signal
  lamp signalling témoins lumineux (signalant l'état d'occupation de chaque ligne)
to sign off terminer, dire au revoir
slot fente
socket prise
software logiciels
sound reproduction reproduction sonore
to speak up parler plus fort
"Speaking." "C'est moi/lui/elle même (à l'appareil)."
standing charge abonnement
STD (Subscriber Trunk Dialling) l'automatique
subscriber abonné
switchboard standard

T

to take (the phone) off the hook décrocher
telecommunications télécommunications
telephone téléphone, appareil
  telephone bill facture du téléphone
  telephone cable câble

telephone credit card carte télécommunications
telephone line ligne téléphonique
cordless telephone téléphone sans cordon

to telephone téléphoner

teleshopping la vente par correspondance sur Minitel

telex telex
telex line ligne telex
telex terminal terminal telex

time charge tarification selon le temps d'utilisation

timer minuteur

tone tonalité
dial tone tonalité (quand on décroche)
ringing tone tonalité (quand le numéro sonne)

transfer facility possibilité de transférer une communication

to transfer transférer

to transmit émettre, diffuser

transmitter poste émetteur

two-digit dialling numérotation abrégée (deux chiffres)

V

videoconference visioconférence

viewdata service service télétel

visual display affichage

W

wire fil

wrong number faux numéro, erreur

Y

Yellow Pages pages jaunes

PHOTOGRAPHS AND ILLUSTATIONS

p. 5: The Financial Times ☐ **p. 6:** British Telecom ☐ **p. 7:** Pix (R. Poinot)
p. 8: British Telecom ☐ **p. 18:** British Telecom ☐ **p. 24:** British Telecom
p. 25: British Telecom ☐ **p. 27:** Punch ☐ **p. 29:** Pix (de Torquat)
p. 34: British Telecom ☐ **p. 38:** Rapho (J-C Bouvier)
p. 39: The Times (Ken Pyne) ☐ **p. 47:** Fotogram (Carol St John)

Achevé d'imprimer sur les presses de Maury-Imprimeur S.A. 45330 Malesherbes
N° d'Édition : 5338 – N° d'Imprimeur : H87/21660 – Dépôt légal : Septembre 1987